second edition

SCHOOLS *and*
DATA

second edition

SCHOOLS
and
DATA

*The Educator's
Guide for
Using Data
to Improve
Decision
Making*

Theodore B.
CREIGHTON

CORWIN PRESS
A SAGE Publications Company
Thousand Oaks, California

For information:

Corwin Press
A Sage Publications Company
2455 Teller Road
Thousand Oaks, California 91320
www.corwinpress.com

Sage Publications Ltd.
1 Oliver's Yard
55 City Road
London EC1Y 1SP
United Kingdom

Sage Publications India Pvt. Ltd.
B-42, Panchsheel Enclave
Post Box 4109
New Delhi 110 017 India

Printed in the United States of America.

Library of Congress Cataloging-in-Publication Data

Creighton, Theodore B.
Schools and data : the educator's guide for using data to improve decision making / Theodore B. Creighton.— 2nd ed.
        p. cm.
Includes bibliographical references and index.
ISBN 1–4129–3732–9 (cloth) — ISBN 1–4129–3733–7 (pbk.)
    1. School management and organization—Statistical methods.
2. Decision making—Statistical methods. I. Title.
LB2805.C737 2007
371.2002′1   2006002986

This book is printed on acid-free paper.

06   07   08   09   10   10   9   8   7   6   5   4   3   2   1

Acquisitions Editor:	Robert D. Clouse
Editorial Assistant:	Jingle Vea
Production Editor:	Jenn Reese
Copy Editor:	Pam Suwinsky
Typesetter:	C&M Digitals (P) Ltd.
Proofreader:	Andrea Martin
Indexer:	Judy Hunt
Cover Designer:	Scott Van Atta
Graphic Designer:	Lisa Miller

Contents

Preface   ix

Acknowledgments   xvii

About the Authors   xix

**1. The Role of Data Analysis in the Lives
   of School Leaders**   1
    What Is This Thing Called Statistics?   2
    What Are SPSS and Excel?   3
    The Rationale for Using Data to Improve
        Decision Making in Our Schools   4
    So, What's the Problem?   4
    The Use of Statistics in the Classroom: A Case Study   5
    Application Activities   7

2. Getting Started   8
    What Is Data-Driven Decision Making?   11
    Introduction to Excel and SPSS   11
    Let's Try an Example   14
    Conclusion   16
    Application Activity   17
    About the NCLB Activities   17

3. Collecting and Organizing Data   19
    Why SPSS and Microsoft Excel?   19
    OK, Let's Give It a Go!   20
    Frequency Distribution   21
    Cross-Tabulation   23
    Measures of Central Tendency   23
    Measures of Variability   27
    Conclusion   29
    Application Activities   30
    NCLB Activity   31

4. Correlation: My GRE Score Is Not Good Enough for Harvard!   **32**
    Why Would Educators Be Interested in Correlations?   38
    A School Music Program: A Case Study   39
    Other Data-Driven Decision Making   45
    Conclusion   46
    Application Activities   49
    NCLB Activity   49

5. Introduction to Regression   **50**
    Simple Regression   52
    Conclusion   61
    Application Activity   62
    NCLB Activity   63

6. Formulating Research Questions and the Comparison of Means   **64**
    Hypothesis Testing and Formulating
      Research Questions   65
    Z Scores   68
    The t Statistic   75
    One-Sample t Test: An Example   77
    Conclusion   79
    Application Activity   80
    NCLB Activity   80

7. The Independent-Samples t Test   **81**
    A Try at Conceptual Understanding   81
    Using SPSS and Excel for Testing
      Independent Samples   93
    OK, Your Turn Now   96
    Conclusion   98
    Application Activity   100
    NCLB Activity   101

8. Analysis of Variance: The Difference Between Two or More Sample Means   **102**
    Advantages of ANOVA Over t Tests   103
    Using the Analysis of Variance   104
    Post Hoc Tests   111
    Conclusion   113

Application Activity 113
NCLB Activity 114

9. Analysis of Variance: Repeated Measures **115**
Let's Get Right to an Example 115
One More Question: Where Does the Difference Lie? 122
Conclusion 124
Application Activity 125
NCLB Activity 126

10. Two-Way Analysis of Variance: Two
Independent Variables **127**
Working With Two Independent Variables 127
Conclusion 134
Application Activity 135
NCLB Activity 135

11. What If No Mean Scores? The Chi-Square
Test for Goodness of Fit **137**
The Chi-Square Formula 139
OK, Let's Practice With a Real-Life Example 141
You're Still With Me? Let's Get Back to the Cafeteria 142
Oops! Let's Check Power and Effect Size 144
Communication of Statistics 145
Conclusion 146
Application Activity 147
NCLB Activity 147

12. The Other "Q" **148**
Getting at the Definition of *Qualitative* 149
OK, but How About a Real-Life Example? 149
Conclusion 152
Application Activity 153
NCLB Activity 153

13. Putting It All Together: An Evidence-Based
Practice Field **155**
Why the Change to Evidence-Based
Decision Making? 156
Practice and Performance Fields 157
An Evidence-Based Practice Field 159
Conclusion 176

Resource A. Music Correlation 179

Resource B. The *t* Distribution Table 180

Resource C. The *F* Distribution Table 182

Resource D. The Chi-Square Distribution Table 184

Resource E. Horizon High School Data 186

References 191

Index 193

Preface

F ew would deny that the main responsibility for the decision-making process in our schools has been assumed by building and central office administrators and that education leaders are now asking (and expecting) classroom teachers to participate in this decision making as well. For too long, many school leaders have made decisions about instructional leadership by using "intuition" and "shooting from the hip." All too often, school leaders do not include data collection and data analysis in the decision-making process.

We are realizing that meaningful information can be gained only from a proper analysis of data and that good decisions are based on this thoughtful process of inquiry and analysis. School districts across the nation collect and maintain many forms of educational data (for example, attendance rates, standardized and criterion-referenced test scores); however, most schools use the collection of these data to satisfy administrative requirements rather than to assess and evaluate school improvement. Educators rarely examine these data to assess in a systematic way the quality of teaching and learning in their schools. This book addresses the dire need for an approach to statistical analysis that is related to educational leadership decision-making applications.

In the first edition of *Schools and Data* (2001), I made the statement that "this need will only become greater as the federal government and our state departments of education ask for more accountability from our school leaders." Here, five years later in 2006, we find that this is exactly what has happened. Though we have made some progress in this regard, the pressure is still on for school leaders to acquire and utilize effective strategies for data collection and analysis. Principals and teachers must possess an understanding and working knowledge of data analysis and ways to use this analysis to improve teaching and learning in the classroom.

Fewer things are more feared than the thought of "statistical analysis." To most educators, *statistics* means endless calculations and memorization of formulas. Statistics is seen by most as a formal domain of advanced mathematics and is represented by a course or two taught by professors who desire to make the student's life as painful as possible. Courses in statistical methods are usually taught with formal proofs of mathematical theorems and the derivation of statistical formulas as a main focus.

Is this anxiety and fear due to the fact that statistical analysis requires a level of mathematical knowledge beyond the capabilities of many principals and teachers? If someone has passed a high school course in elementary algebra, he or she has acquired all the knowledge and skills required for an understanding of statistical analysis (Runyan, Haber, & Coleman, 1994). Students report that their fear is mostly related to the fact that statistics has no relevance to solving the many issues in our day-to-day living (Creighton, 1999).

The educator's fear of statistics probably relates to a variety of factors, but teacher and principal preparation programs must accept that the presentation of statistics in education probably lacks four important components. First, it does not emphasize the relevance of statistics to the day-to-day lives of principals and teachers. Second, it does not fully integrate current technology into the teaching and learning of statistics. Third, few (if any) statistics courses are designed for students enrolled in teacher education or education leadership programs. Fourth, and finally, many statistics courses taught in colleges of education devote a major part of their time to inferential statistics as a tool in conducting research projects and dissertations. Far less time is spent on statistical strategies that might help the principal or teacher improve their skills in problem analysis, program and student evaluation, data-based decision making, and report preparation (McNamara, 1996).

The second edition of *Schools and Data: The Educator's Guide for Using Data to Improve Decision Making* addresses these four issues. A brief description of each follows.

RELEVANCE OF STATISTICS TO THE LIVES OF PRINCIPALS AND TEACHERS

Traditional courses in statistics result in the frequent student response: "When will I ever use this stuff?" This book provides examples, data sets, and problems centered on a wide range of real-world data distributions used by principals and teachers in their work in schools. In addition, real-life examples completed by principals and teachers in the field are presented in most chapters.

Integration of Recent Technology Into the Teaching and Learning of Statistics

The teaching of applied educational statistics needs to move away from the common perception of statistics as mathematical theory and closer to teacher and principal preparation programs (McNamara, 1996). The advances in technology and the large selection of user-friendly computer software can now assist us as we make this move toward a more practical and relevant presentation of statistics for educators. Though several good statistical packages exist, two leading statistical packages are mentioned throughout this book: (1) Statistical Package for the Social Sciences (SPSS), and (2) Microsoft Excel. Both are easy-to-use, menu-driven statistical programs applicable for analyzing such data as student standardized test scores, attendance and dropout rates, and college entrance requirements. A "student version" of SPSS costs less than $100 and is powerful enough to handle any analysis encountered in schools or the university classroom. I include Microsoft Excel because it also is a very powerful software for data analysis and it is likely already to be on your computer or laptop.

Though we agree with the importance of educators' learning to calculate statistics, the early and regular use of SPSS and/or Excel allows the student and practitioner to spend less time on complex mathematical calculations and more time on statistical selection and interpretation. It is important to state that research and statistics have less to do with the collection and analysis of data, and more to do with the interpretation and meaning of the analysis. Step-by-step procedures are presented in each chapter of this book, accompanied by real-world applications to educators' problems in the field. The procedures and examples are also available as interactive simulations and demonstrations on the *Schools and Data* Web site, available at: http://www.schoolsanddata.org. The data sets presented in the chapters and the Resources at the end of the book are also posted on the Web site and can be easily downloaded for your use.

Statistical Analysis Designed for Educators

This second edition of *Schools and Data* centers on both master's and doctoral-level research and statistics courses taught in the Department of Educational Leadership and the Center for Research and Doctoral Studies in Educational Leadership at Sam Houston State University. Many of the examples included in each chapter are projects and studies conducted by practicing teachers and principals working on master's or doctoral degrees. The data are collected from real classrooms, focusing on student instruction and assessment; attendance, dropout, and graduation rates; college entrance tests; and instructional program evaluations.

Descriptive and Inferential Statistics

First, I want to state that we need to guard against the notion that descriptive data and analysis are less powerful than inferential analysis. Inferential statistics are methods that use sample data to make generalizations about the population. In most cases, we simply want to study the situations in our schools. Rarely do we want to make generalizations about other schools or students. For example, if we are studying the effect of whole language instruction in our fourth grade classrooms, we are not interested in fourth graders across the country—we only want to know what is happening with *our* fourth grade students. Though inferential statistics is a useful tool, descriptive analysis can be just as powerful. Think for a moment about the book written by Jonathan Kozol entitled *Savage Inequalities* (1992). As you know, it is a book about the inequities in our large urban schools. Kozol's research was purely descriptive—he used no complex statistical analysis, he just *described and reported* what he observed in the city schools he wrote about. The point is important here: Kozol's book was of great impact and very influential not only in the realization of our inattention to our urban schools and children, but it also made a great impact on educators and society as a whole and was instrumental in the restructuring of our large urban schools. I suggest that no amount of inferential analysis could have had such a significant effect.

Though inferential statistics are more likely to be used in research studies and dissertations, descriptive statistics are more likely to be used in schools. Descriptive statistics (percentile ranks, means, median, modes, range, standard deviation) help us *describe* those studied, and inferential statistics use sample data to *estimate* parameters and test hypotheses. In most cases, the educator encounters data in the schools that are related to populations rather than to samples. In other words, data are collected from entire classes or grade levels, entire building populations, or entire district populations. Principals and teachers are not especially interested in generalizing their school data findings to other schools or estimating parameters and testing hypotheses.

Though much of this book's emphasis will be on descriptive data collection and analysis, I include many examples of how the educator can use inferential statistical analysis. But I attempt to shift the use of inferential analysis from the traditional research and dissertation model to one of relevance and applicability to teachers and administrators.

THE SECOND EDITION

Effective Leaders Needed

The challenges we face in schools today are increasing, and never before has the importance of using data and evidence to make decisions about school improvement and increasing student achievement been so crucial. But these challenges have changed somewhat from our challenges of the past decade—new standards, emphasis on new accountability, and the frequent charges from our stakeholders (federal, state, and local) that schools are not performing at high levels. And because these challenges have changed, there is a need to revisit the processes we use in program evaluation and data analysis. This second edition of *Schools and Data* addresses these new challenges and presents new processes for school leaders to provide the leadership necessary for school improvement and increased student learning.

The revisions to the second edition of *Schools and Data* are based on feedback received from school leaders (for example, principals, superintendents, teachers), and university professors and graduate students who use the book in their classes. Specifically, the revisions include a change in the format of the text, the creation of four new chapters, and the inclusions of several new features.

The New Format

Theoretical Framework

Due to the increased focus on standards and accountability, I have designed many of the application activities around the federal legislation No Child Left Behind (NCLB). This legislation serves as a framework for the second edition.

Inclusion of New Statistical Software

Though I continue to use examples and data sets utilizing the Statistical Package for the Social Sciences (SPSS), I parallel SPSS with Microsoft Excel, assuming that many of my readers have easy access to Excel, a very powerful data analysis tool in its own right.

Four New Chapters

New chapters were added for two reasons: (1) important topics were missing from the first edition, and (2) the total of 13 chapters better fits into a traditional semester course, allowing for the study and reflection of one chapter per week.

Chapter 5: Introduction to Regression

As an extension of correlation, regression helps us investigate relationships between variables much further than just determining strength and direction of the relationship. Regression allows us to determine what type of relationship exists and what kinds of predictions we can make from the relationship.

Chapter 11: What If No Mean Scores? The Chi-Square Test for Goodness of Fit

All of the tests presented in the first edition involved numerical scores (for example, test scores) for each individual in the sample. These tests are called *parametric tests* because they all make certain assumptions about our samples—that the distributions are normal (you know, the normal curve) and that there are equal variances among our different groups.

Often (actually very often), school leaders are confronted with situations that do not conform to the assumptions or requirements of parametric tests. For example, let's suppose we are interested in analyzing the number of students who pass versus the students who fail our state's required assessment. Our students will be really just classified into two categories (pass or fail). A student is either one or the other (kind of a label or category).

Fortunately, there is a hypothesis-testing technique that provides an alternative to parametric tests. This alternative is called a *nonparametric test*—or formally, the chi-square test. There is no need to get technical here (or, as you may recall from my first edition, maybe there is never a need to get technical), but I point out here that the difference between *parametric* and *nonparametric* relates to the type of data we are using. All of the data sets used in the first edition of *Schools and Data* involved numerical scores (interval data). For *nonparametric tests*, on the other hand, our subjects are usually just classified into categories or frequencies (nominal data). Chapter 11 in this new edition covers the chi-square test thoroughly and demonstrates its usefulness in improving schools and student achievement.

Chapter 12: The Other "Q"

Perhaps my friends and colleagues will be surprised to hear me state that few, if any, evaluations and assessments in our schools would be complete without some qualitative information. For example, the qualitative technique of "observation" is essential for just about every evaluation we conduct in our schools—observing student behavior, observing teacher performance, and many others. Another qualitative technique, the "interview," is useful when greater depth in information is needed. When we sit down with all the fifth grade teachers to discuss programmatic issues, we really are utilizing a qualitative technique called "focus groups." Valuable data comes from these and other qualitative strategies. Chapter 12 in this second edition presents the importance of adding qualitative methods to our use of data to improve decision making in our schools.

Chapter 13: Putting It All Together: An Evidence-Based Practice Field

Fortunately, the recent emphasis on accountability requires us to look more closely at existing data as we make our decisions toward school improvement. *Unfortunately,* and cause for alarm, is that in our haste to collect and analyze existing data, we have neglected to investigate beyond existing data to consider "below the surface" data. The cause for alarm relates to the fact that many of our special needs students (for example, limited-English speakers, students of color, students with disabilities) are not served well when we only examine surface data. Chapter 13 of the second edition introduces the practice of using *evidence* (below the surface) as opposed to just considering *existing data* (surface).

New End-of-the-Chapter Features

New Application Activities

Chapters 1–12 conclude with updated and relevant opportunities to practice application. The activities are a blend of elementary, middle, and high school examples and scenarios.

NCLB Application Activities

Chapters 3–12 each have a specific activity related to the goals and requirements of the No Child Left Behind legislation.

The *Schools and Data* Companion Web Site

The author has created a special Web site, available at: http://www.schoolsanddata.org, to provide additional information and that contains activities paralleling the individual chapters of the second edition of *Schools and Data*. For example, school leaders and graduate students can view interactive simulations and demonstrations that include audio, animation, and interactions. The Web site also includes sample syllabi for university professors in principal preparation programs. These simulations are in both SPSS and Excel formats. Most important, this site has a question-and-answer forum that allows principals, teachers, students, and professors to communicate directly with the author. In addition, PowerPoint presentations have been developed on key concepts of each chapter containing the tables and figures from that chapter. These syllabi, presentations, simulations, and demonstrations are free to use and can be easily downloaded for your work in schools and classrooms.

Acknowledgments

Someone once stated that an author is essentially the pen through which significant others write. In this case, the significant others are the many education leaders I have met in my master's and doctoral classes at two universities. Though I only mention a few in this book, I am grateful to all of the master's and doctoral students at the university who helped me turn this thing called "statistics" into a meaningful and comprehensible experience for our aspiring and practicing teachers and administrators.

The creation of tables and figures is a critical component of a book such as this. Youfeng Nie, a master's student in educational leadership, deserves my thanks for a job well done. Youfeng also provided me with his expertise in analyzing data with Microsoft Excel. He appropriately is a *contributing author* of this second edition of *Schools and Data*.

PUBLISHER'S ACKNOWLEDGMENTS

Corwin Press gratefully acknowledges the contributions of the following individuals:

Bess Sullivan Scott
Principal
Goodrich Middle
    School
Lincoln, NE

Erin A. Rivers
Principal
DeLaSalle Middle School
Mission, KS

Deborah Johnson
Principal
Lunt School
Falmouth, NE

Rosemarie I. Young
Principal, NAESP President
Watson Lane Elementary
    School
Louisville, KY

Judith A. Smith
Regional System of District
    and School Support
Division of School
    Improvement
Los Angeles County Office
    of Education
Los Angeles, CA

Kathleen G. Hood
Curriculum Director
Spearfish School District
    #402
Spearfish, SD

Sue Pedro
Director of Elementary
    Curriculum and
    Instruction
Washington Local Schools
Toledo, OH

Charol Shakeshaft
Managing Director,
    Interactive Inc.
Professor
Foundations, Leadership
    and Policy Studies
Hofstra University
Hempstead, NY

Jimmy Byrd
Assistant Professor
Educational
    Administration,
    Counseling and
    Psychology
Tarleton State University
Stephenville, TX

Elaine M. Walker
Associate Professor
Educational Leadership,
    Management and Policy
Seton Hall University
South Orange, NJ

Miriam S. Grosof
Professor Emerita of
    Mathematics
Yeshiva University
New York, NY

Kay Davis
Professor
GSEP
Pepperdine University
West Los Angeles, CA

About the Authors

Theodore B. Creighton is currently Professor and Program Leader in the Department of Educational Leadership and Policy Studies at Virginia Tech. Prior to joining the faculty at Virginia Tech, he served as Director of the Center for Research and Doctoral Studies in Educational Leadership at Sam Houston State University and as a Professor in Educational Leadership at Idaho State University. His background includes teaching at all grade levels in Washington, D.C.; Cleveland, Ohio; and Los Angeles, California. His administrative experience includes serving as a principal and superintendent in both Fresno and Kern Counties, California. He holds a BS degree in teacher education from Indiana University of Pennsylvania, a master's degree in educational administration from California State University Long Beach, and a doctorate from the University of California Davis. Though active in many professional organizations, he devotes considerable time to his role as Executive Director of the National Council of Professors of Educational Administration. He also serves as a member of the National Policy Board for Educational Administration (NPBEA), and as a Stafford Faculty Fellow for the National Institute on Leadership, Disabilities and Students Placed at Risk (NILDSPAR). He recently was appointed as Project Director of the Connexions Knowledge Base Project, an international initiative in collaboration with Rice University charged with assembling the knowledge base in educational administration. His research includes examining the forces of the school principalship, and he is widely published in the area of schools with alternative forms of school leadership. His most recent

Corwin Press publications are *The Principal as Technology Leader* (2003) and *Leading From Below the Surface* (2005).

Youfeng Nie, contributing author, is a graduate student at Sam Houston State University. Nie is an international student with school leadership experience in China, and has just completed a master's degree in Educational Administration. He currently is completing a second master's degree in Statistics Science, and has applied to several prestigious doctoral programs around the country. He will be an asset to the profession.

CHAPTER ONE

The Role of Data Analysis in the Lives of School Leaders

D uring my many years as a classroom teacher and then as a principal and superintendent of schools, I often questioned the enormous amount of time we spent in collecting numbers. Thirty to 40 minutes each morning were spent in collecting and reporting attendance. The annual state-mandated testing procedure began in early October and seemed to continue in one form or another for the entire year. But we collected our scores, sent them to the office, and never saw them again.

School districts across the nation collect and maintain many forms of educational data. Standardized test scores, average daily attendance figures, and transcript data are required by states for funding purposes. However, most schools use the collection of these data to satisfy administrative requirements rather than to assess and evaluate school improvement. Standardized test scores are generally reviewed only briefly before the local newspaper calls. Of course, this has changed somewhat since the first edition of *Schools and Data,* now that test scores are being used as a yardstick to measure teacher and principal performance. Interestingly, although we are spending more time with data and analyses, we are in most cases responding to directives and legislation (U.S. Department of Education, 2001). We are being reactive, not proactive. We must become much more proactive and move beyond the "on the surface" work with data—and investigate "below the surface" issues related to our data. The evidence reveals that many schools report such things as *average daily attendance* to their state departments (for reimbursement), then file the information away someplace. Educators rarely examine these data to assess *in a systematic way* the quality of teaching and learning at their schools (MPR Associates, 1998).

What Is This Thing Called Statistics?

First of all, statistics is not advanced mathematics. The majority of statistical analyses useful to the principal and teacher can be completed with a basic understanding of mathematics and involve conceptual understanding rather than complex calculations and formulas. Statistics is a set of tools designed to help *describe* the sample or population from which the data were gathered and to *explain* the possible relationship between variables.

A school principal wonders if the mathematics instruction in her school is being delivered in a manner that is not biased toward either boys or girls. In other words, Is mathematics being presented in an equitable manner at her school? A simple statistical procedure called the *Pearson correlation* can help identify any existing relationships between math scores and gender (this procedure, along with the Statistical Package for the Social Sciences [SPSS] and Excel steps to conduct it, is presented in Chapter 4). If the analysis indicates that there is a pattern of boys receiving high scores on standardized tests more than girls, the principal may want to look more closely at classroom instruction to determine if instructional strategies can be altered to address this equity issue.

A seventh grade language arts teacher is interested in knowing if there is a relationship between students' performance on the district writing assessment and their socioeconomic level. In other words, do students who come from lower socioeconomic backgrounds *really* perform at lower levels, as we are led to believe? Or, are other variables responsible for the variance in writing performance? Again, a simple correlation analysis will help *describe* the students' performance and help *explain* the relationship between the issues of performance and socioeconomic level.

Data analysis does not have to involve complex statistics. Data analysis in schools involves (1) collecting data and (2) using available data for the purpose of improving teaching and learning. Interesting enough, principals and teachers have it pretty easy—in most cases the collection of data has already been completed. Schools regularly collect attendance data, transcript records, quarterly and semester grades, state and national standardized test scores, and a variety of other useful data. Generally, we are interested not so much in complex statistical formulas and tests as we are in simple counts, averages, percentages, and rates. We cover more of this later.

WHAT ARE SPSS AND EXCEL?

Statistical Package for the Social Sciences and Microsoft Excel are common computer software programs that can allow people in the social sciences to analyze their data. Most educators and students in university programs have access to SPSS, and I suspect those of you in schools have access to Microsoft Excel. Good, complete versions of SPSS and Excel are reasonably priced. SPSS is now offered in a student version for $90, and, obviously, Excel is part of the Microsoft Office Suites software loaded on most of our office and home computers. True, SPSS is a more thorough set of analysis tools, but Excel is just fine for most of the analyses we discuss and cover in *Schools and Data*. Therefore, I include examples of both programs throughout the chapters and on the accompanying Web site for the book at: http://www.schoolsanddata.org.

Both of these software programs can tabulate the numbers of males and females in a school, calculate average grades of the students, compare test scores by gender, determine if there is a statistically significant difference between athletes and nonathletes, compare computer-assisted instruction with other methods of delivery, and so on. SPSS and Excel display frequency distributions and cross-tabulations and calculate descriptive statistics (mean, mode, median, range, interquartile range, standard deviation) in addition to inferential statistics (chi-square, Pearson correlation, t tests, regression, and so on). *Schools and Data* uses both programs throughout the book for examples and illustrations. And, becoming familiar with these two software programs will not be a disadvantage to individuals who end up in schools that use other computer software programs (for example, Minitab, SAS).

THE RATIONALE FOR USING DATA TO IMPROVE DECISION MAKING IN OUR SCHOOLS

Much research and evidence now exist indicating why school leaders must become familiar with and use existing school data to make sound educational decisions about teaching and learning (Fitch & Malcom, 1998; McNamara, 1996; Picciano, 2005; U.S. Department of Education, 2001). The National Science Foundation and the National Center for Educational Statistics have developed an information management and data-warehousing system that provides school leaders with easy-to-use access to all of their data (available at: http://nces.ed.gov/). The system focuses on how best to use these technologies for effective school leadership and improved decision making. Anthony Picciano (2005) from Hunter College, City University of New York, has published an excellent book entitled *Data-Driven Decision Making for Effective School Leadership*, which provides a theoretical background and practical considerations for planning and implementing data-driven decision-making processes in schools and school districts.

The question I hope this second edition of *Schools and Data* answers is, "What aspects of statistical methods should be emphasized in a basic statistics course that is designed explicitly to help school leaders (principals *and* teachers) improve their skills in problem analysis, program evaluation, evidence-based decision making, and program preparation?"

SO, WHAT'S THE PROBLEM?

Edie Holcomb's very successful book (now in its second edition), *Getting Excited About Data* (2005), discusses why data are little used in our schools and why it is so difficult to generate passion to get educators engaged:

> My observations are that more than half of our teachers have graduate degrees and have taken at least one course in tests and measurements or statistics. I have four graduate degrees myself and can recall no class discussion of what to do with assessment information in planning how to help students do better. I have come to the conclusions that such courses are taught by researchers as though they are preparing researchers. As a

result, the emphasis is on esoteric experimental design—which can't be replicated in a normal school setting. (Holcomb, 2005, p. 22)

Holcomb continues by quoting Gerald Bracey (1997), internationally recognized as one of the country's most respected experts in the understanding of education statistics:

Many of the university professors who create and use statistics are more comfortable using them than they are teaching other human beings what they mean. And in all too many instances, statistics are taught in a theoretically rarefied atmosphere replete with hard-to-understand formulas and too few examples of the daily life of education practitioners. (Holcomb, 2005, p. 22)

I agree with Holcomb and also state that the uses of data suggested in this book are not likely to meet the academic standards required in dissertations. The book's purpose is to illustrate how statistical analysis can be applied to everyday situations found in our schools. This book can be used as a refresher for all educators who have had some courses in applied statistics or research but have never found a way to use what they were taught. Let's get started.

THE USE OF STATISTICS IN THE CLASSROOM: A CASE STUDY

Karla, who taught Grades 3 and 4 mathematics at a small rural school district in southeastern Idaho, was interested in finding out if a mathematics series adopted by the district 5 years earlier was effective for all levels of students. Karla's research question was:

Though the district math program seems to be effective with middle- and low-ability students, why are the students with above-average ability not showing similar gains?

Her interest and question were based upon the belief that the district math program overemphasized computation and repetition but lacked the components of in-depth investigations and problem-solving experiences. To help answer her question, she collected 4 years of Iowa Test of Basic Skills (ITBS) percentile rank scores on her students. She created the following procedures:

Step 1. Rank the students into categories of high, medium, and low. Karla based her grouping on the percentile rank scores from the first-year baseline data and categorized students scoring at or above the 60th percentile as the high group, students scoring at or above the 40th but below the 60th percentile as the medium group, and students scoring below the 40th percentile as the low group.

Step 2. Create a data file. Using SPSS for Windows, Karla entered the students' ITBS percentile ranks into a new SPSS file.

Step 3. Analyze the data. With a few simple mouse clicks on her computer, she discovered that:

a. All (100%) of her students who were rated "below average" increased their scores over the 4-year period.

b. An unusually high number (75%) of her students who were rated "above average" revealed a general decline in their scores over the same 4-year period.

After running a few more statistical tests (descriptive) with her student data, Karla presented her findings to her principal and superintendent. She was invited to share her data analysis with the board of education. Though realizing that her analysis did not prove anything, Karla felt that the discovered pattern indicated a need for reevaluating the math program and especially her teaching methods in the classroom. Karla's conclusion to the superintendent and board was that the district math program seemed to be challenging the lower-level students by reinforcing basic skills, but the higher level of students (having already mastered the fundamentals) needed additional instruction to apply, inquire, and experiment with the numbers and mathematical concepts they already knew.

The end of the story was the implementation by Karla and her colleagues of an enrichment math program that encouraged the higher-level students to think mathematically, apply this thinking to more complex and multidimensional math problems, and communicate this thinking clearly.

Complex statistical analysis? Not really! Sound education decision making? I would argue so!

APPLICATION ACTIVITIES

1. Take an informal tour of your building office and the central office in your school district. Make a list of all the different kinds of data your district collects (for example, standardized and performance-based test scores and attendance, dropout, and graduate rates). Make special note of the data that seem to go nowhere. In other words, how much of what your district collects is done to satisfy state and federal requirements and then is merely filed away someplace?

2. Review this statement from the Preface: "The educator's fear of statistics probably relates to a variety of factors, but teacher and principal preparation programs must accept that the presentation of statistics in education probably lacks four important components." What advice would you offer to those of us who are responsible for teacher and administrator preparation programs at the university level? How might we better address data analysis in our preparation programs? Do you feel that this "fear of statistics" really exists, and if so, can the fear be reduced or eliminated?

3. Access the Internet, and visit the *Schools and Data* Web site at: http://www.schoolsanddata.org. Become familiar with the site and the resources available to you. You are invited to communicate with the author and share your responses to the questions asked in Activity #2.

CHAPTER TWO

Getting Started

Assuming that you are still a bit nervous about the "S" word, and perhaps still unconvinced that teachers and principals can use statistics easily to help with the day-to-day decisions we need to make, let's look at a simple example of how statistics can be used to improve student achievement. We start with a statistic all of us are comfortable with already—percentages. Table 2.1 describes a tenth grade English class involved in a study.

There are a total of 122 students in tenth grade at Westside High School, with 10 more males than females (54% − 46% = 8% of 122 = 9.76 or 10). We use percentages every day to describe our average daily attendance (ADA), students receiving "free and reduced lunch," number of teachers with advanced degrees, and so on. Let's use this same statistic and add some other statistical information—Iowa Test of Basic Skills (ITBS) scores—to further describe our group (Table 2.2).

Remember, percentile ranks give us a picture of where students are scoring when compared to national averages. We see that 11 females scored in the 25th percentile, with only 6 males scoring at that rank. We now have a clearer picture of our tenth graders and their achievement level in mathematics. A greater number of our female students are scoring in the 25th and 50th percentiles. In addition, more of our male students are scoring at a higher level (that is, 50th and 75th percentiles). Does this *prove* that boys are smarter than girls in mathematics? Of course not! But our data show a pattern that warrants a closer look at what is happening in our tenth grade math curriculum. Actually, we should look at

Table 2.1   Gender of Westside High School Tenth Graders

Gender	Number of Students	Percentage (%) of Total
Female	56	46
Male	66	54

Table 2.2   Westside High School Tenth Graders' ITBS Math Percentile Ranks by Gender ($N = 122$)

	Females	Males
25th percentile	11	6
50th percentile	30	20
75th percentile	10	30
99th percentile	5	10

several previous grades to determine if the same pattern exists over time. Our classroom instruction and activities may show favoritism toward the male students. Our entire mathematics faculty may be male and may demonstrate an unknowing and unconscious instructional delivery weighted toward the male students. Or none of the above may be the case, and some entirely different variables may be at work (for example, more females may be limited English speaking). However, the pattern in test scores forces us to take a closer look at our curriculum, teaching, and assessment. This leads us to *data-driven decision making*. Before we look specifically at data-driven decision making, let's look at one more example of analyzing some of the data that exist in our schools.

As administrators, we are all familiar with collecting average daily attendance figures. These numbers provide the formula used to receive our funding from the state and federal governments. In most cases, once we report these numbers to our county office or state department, we put the data away in a file someplace. Rarely do we use these data to make decisions about curriculum and instruction. Let's return to Westside High School and look at their average daily attendance rates for 2000, 2001, and 2002. These data are displayed in Table 2.3.

Table 2.3   Average Daily Attendance at Westside High School

Year	Percentage (%) Attending
2000	94
2001	92
2002	94

At first glance, things look impressive. On average, over a 3-year period, 93% of our students are in school every day. We reason that 93% is kind of like an "A" and is pretty good. So we report the figures to the appropriate agencies and move on with life. But let's take a closer look. If 93% of our students are in attendance on average, we must conclude that 7% of our students are absent on average. So in fact, on average, our high school students miss nearly 2 weeks of school each year. We calculate this by taking 7% of the 180 school days ($180 \times .07 = 12.60$). Wow! Now that's a different story. Do we not agree that missing 13 days of school (on average) has curriculum and instruction ramifications? Are there ways of adjusting our curriculum, scheduling, and delivery of instruction that might help us reduce the number of absences at Westside High School? Let's *disaggregate* or break our data down a bit further. Table 2.4 displays our attendance rate on a daily basis.

Now we see a different picture! With no great surprise, we notice an up-and-down attendance pattern during the week. But when looking at our curriculum, scheduling, and extracurricular activities, we notice that the highest attendance rate is on

Table 2.4   Westside High School Attendance on a Daily Basis

Day	Percentage (%) Attending
Monday	95
Tuesday	95
Wednesday	97
Thursday	91
Friday	89

Wednesday—the day we hold our football rally! In addition, we notice our lowest attendance rate is on Friday—the day most of our testing and assessment takes place! Perhaps the principal should consider changing the football rally to Friday and encourage the teachers to do more of their testing on other days.

These examples illustrate how easy it is to use existing data to help us with the day-to-day operation of our schools. My hope is that you will feel a bit more at ease with the approach this book takes in demonstrating to principals and teachers the use of data analysis and how we link data analysis to what we spend our lives with—curriculum, instruction, assessment, and student achievement.

What Is Data-Driven Decision Making?

Collecting data without purpose is meaningless. All too often, school leaders fail to formulate decisions based on data. The effective use of data must play a major role in the development of school improvement plans (Fitch & Malcom, 1998). Too many of our school leaders make decisions based on "informed intuition." Meaningful information can be gained only from a proper analysis of data.

Using the many different kinds of data collected at our school sites to help with decision making legitimizes the goals and strategies we create for change and improvement. It helps us identify groups of students who are improving and groups of students who are not—and helps to identify the reasons. Thus, the principal can serve as instructional leader. Data-driven decision making and instructional leadership must go hand in hand.

Introduction to Excel and SPSS

Earlier in the chapter, we discovered that a simple descriptive statistic such as percentages can help us answer many questions about our school and students. Does statistical analysis get any harder than this? Yes, perhaps! However, with the help of advanced statistical software packages such as Excel and Statistical Package for the Social Sciences (SPSS), there is no longer a need to understand advanced mathematical formulas—or use them, for that matter. Most statistical analysis is as easy as pointing and clicking. Yes, first we must conceptually understand what we are doing. We must realize that computer statistical software merely gives numerical answers and saves the time and effort of doing calculations by hand. We are still responsible for understanding and interpreting each statistical concept.

Getting Started With Excel

Microsoft Excel has the capability to solve most statistical problems addressed in this book. However, you must make sure you have access to the Data Analysis Add-in. Here is the procedure for doing so; the steps are posted on the schoolsanddata.org Web site. To activate the Data Analysis Add-in:

1. Select **Tools** on the Excel Worksheet menu bar.

2. Select **Add-Ins** from the **Tools** menu.

3. Check the box for **Analysis ToolPak**.

A screenshot of the Excel Add-Ins box appears as Figure 2.1.

Figure 2.1   Loading Excel ToolPak

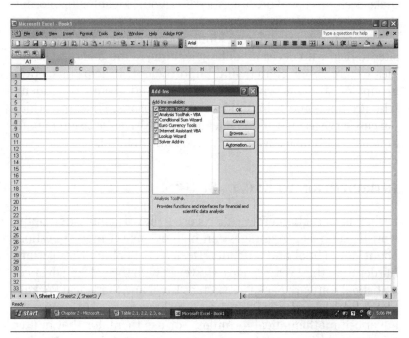

Visit http://www.schoolsanddata.org to view a simulation of the procedure for activating the Data Analysis Add-In.

Entering Data With Excel

1. Click the cell at the top of the column where you want to enter data. When working with values for a single variable, enter the values into a column.

2. Type each data value and press **Enter** or **Tab.**

3. You can also download data sets from other files by simply copying from the existing file and pasting into Excel. We cover more on this function later.

Getting Started With SPSS

Using SPSS for Windows is very similar to the procedures presented for Excel. After entering the Windows environment, use the mouse to select (point and click once) the **SPSS for Windows** icon. When you open SPSS, a slightly different screen appears. The menu shown in Figure 2.2 will appear on your monitor.

Figure 2.2   SPSS Opening Dialogue Box

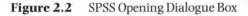

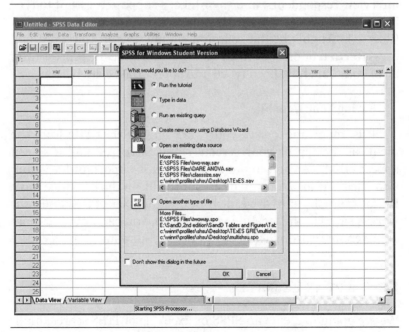

To begin with, you may want to select **Run the tutorial** and click on **Open.** Several options appear that will assist you in touring the SPSS program. Enjoy!

Creating an SPSS Data File

Going back to the menu in Figure 2.2, select **Type in data**, and an empty spreadsheet will appear. You are now ready to input data from your classroom, office, or school.

Labeling Variables

Variables are named in the columns across the top of the SPSS spreadsheet. To give each a name (for example, itbsmath, itbsread, or itbsscie), double-click on the cell labeled **VAR**. A dialogue box will appear that allows you to name your column (limit of eight characters). Click **OK,** and you return to your data spreadsheet. Continue double-clicking on the separate columns until you have all your variables named.

Entering Your Data

The spreadsheet rows are in numerical order and can be used to represent your sample (for example, individual students, classes, interview respondents, and so on). Let's suppose we want to type in the Iowa Test of Basic Skills math score for our first student (Row #1). Highlight the cell, and simply type in the score and press **Return** or one of the arrow keys. Continue the process until all of your data have been typed into appropriate cells.

Saving Your Data File

It is important to save your work often. Select **File** from the menu at the top of your screen, select **Save As,** and a screen appears that asks you to name the file. It is important for you to also select the location you desire for the file in the box titled **Save In** (for example, hard drive, disk, or desktop). Select **OK**, and your work is saved in the location you selected. You can now add more data, rename existing variables, or begin your data analysis.

LET'S TRY AN EXAMPLE

We are going to create an SPSS or Excel file of ITBS scores (math and reading) for a class of sixth graders to determine if there might be a correlation between the students' math and reading scores.

In other words, we want to see if students who have a tendency to score high in math also tend to score high in reading (positive correlation). Of course, we might find out that an opposite pattern exists—students who score high in math tend to score low in reading (negative correlation). If either of these conditions exists, perhaps we can help demonstrate to our teachers the importance of collaborative instructional strategies across the two disciplines. We may also want to investigate other reasons for the relationship between these two variables. While we are collecting these data, we might want to note the gender of each student so we can look at the relationship between achievement and gender. To simplify the process, for example, we use data from only five students. The data are shown in Table 2.5.

Table 2.5   Sixth Graders' ITBS Math and Reading Scores by Gender

Student Number	Gender	Math Score	Reading Score
1	Female	230	222
2	Male	245	230
3	Female	210	200
4	Male	235	235
5	Male	220	215

There is really no need to insert the student numbers of 1–5, as we can use the numbered grid already showing on the SPSS spreadsheet. So, our first column would be labeled *gender,* second column *math,* and third column *reading.* Just be aware that SPSS and Excel work better with numbers than words. You will want to come up with some numbers to represent the words *male* and *female.* It is traditional to use the numbers 1 and 2 or 0 and 1. For example, let's assign the number 1 to represent *female* and the number 2 to represent *male.* Not to worry—trust me, computers are pretty dumb and only understand numbers. Oops, one more thing—when you are labeling your variables (columns), you will want to change the decimal in SPSS to 0, as it is set for two decimal places. Other times, such as when you're using grade point average

(GPA), you will want to keep the two-place decimal setting (for example, GPA = 2.45). Figure 2.3 shows what the file should look like in both SPSS and Excel.

Figure 2.3   Data View

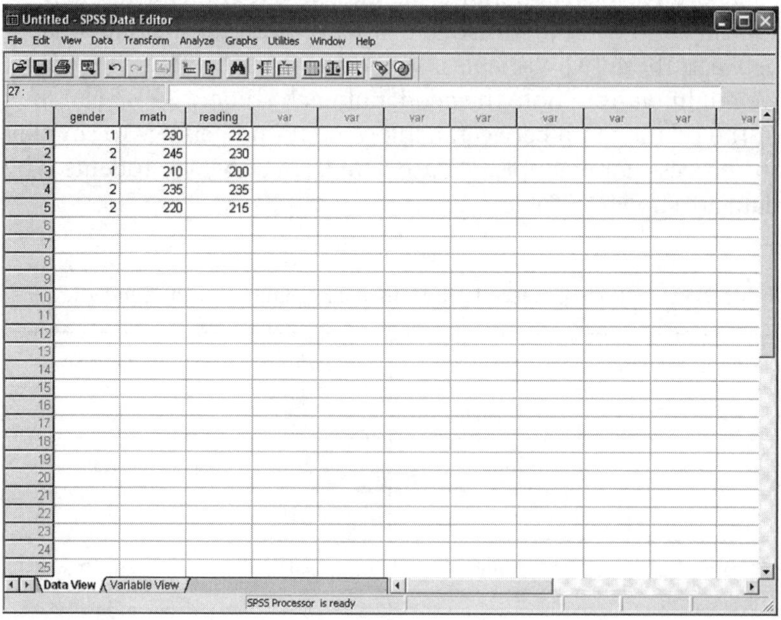

CONCLUSION

You will hear me say several times throughout this book that we must be careful not to move too quickly into the use of computer software to analyze our data. The reason for this caution relates to the importance of first conceptualizing and understanding what our questions are and what we are investigating. This thinking is helpful in making sure we have the data entered correctly and we are using the appropriate analysis tool. Now, having said this, let me say I also agree that we are increasingly provided with excellent computer software that makes calculations for us very quickly.

My particular excitement about the new computer software is that it allows us to spend less time on calculations and formulas and more time with analysis and interpretation. We can now concern ourselves with the actual problems at hand and looking for practical solutions to them. In Chapter 3, we begin to work with some real-life school data. Press on!

APPLICATION ACTIVITY

Using either SPSS or Excel, open a new data file. Let's practice with inputting 10 students, along with their gender, ethnicity, and math scores. Code the different ethnicity options with numbers as we did with gender in Table 2.5. So, you might use 1 to represent Hispanic, 2 to represent Asian, 3 to represent Black, and 4 to represent White. Now, practice *saving* the file to your desktop, and *save* again to disk or CD. Just for fun, try *copying* all the cells (by highlighting all the cells with your mouse) with the **Copy** function under the **File** menu—and open up a new file, select a cell, and *paste*. Get it?

ABOUT THE NCLB ACTIVITIES

Yikes, what's this? As mentioned in the preface, I include an activity or two at the end of each chapter (beginning with Chapter 3) related to the No Child Left Behind (NCLB) legislation. Obviously, much of our time in schools is spent with the directives included in this federal regulation. As you know, NCLB was signed into law January 8, 2002. It is the latest revision of the 1965 Elementary and Secondary Education Act (ESEA) and is regarded as the most significant education policy initiative in a generation.

The overall purpose of the law is to ensure that each child in America is able to meet the high learning standards of the state where he or she lives. Here are the specific goals of the law, as spelled out in the *Federal Register* issued on March 6, 2002:

1. All students will reach high standards, at a minimum attaining proficiency or better in reading and mathematics by 2013–2014.

2. By 2013–2014, all students will be proficient in reading by the end of third grade.

3. All limited English proficient students will become proficient in English.

4. By 2005–2006, all students will be taught by highly qualified teachers.

5. All students will be educated in learning environments that are safe, drug-free, and conducive to learning.

6. All students will graduate from high school. (U.S. Department of Education, 2001)

So, you see—we have our work cut out for us. I am hopeful that *Schools and Data* will be helpful to us all as we strive to help our schools and districts meet these goals. Beginning with Chapter 3 of *Schools and Data*, specific NCLB activities are included at the end of each chapter.

CHAPTER THREE

Collecting and Organizing Data

WHY SPSS AND MICROSOFT EXCEL?

My intended audience for *Schools and Data* includes both college professors and school practitioners. Obviously, most university professors and students have access to and a working knowledge of Statistical Package for the Social Sciences (SPSS). On the other hand, many school practitioners have Excel—a readily accessible program and probably the most commonly used spreadsheet—at their fingertips. It seems practical and reasonable to demonstrate these two software packages. Therefore, I make a general recommendation for the practitioners to consider using Excel (unless they have access to SPSS) and for the university folks to use SPSS.

I would be remiss if I did not point out that Excel has some limitations and may not be the best choice for some statistical analyses. Most important to know is that data organization in Excel differs according to analysis, forcing you to reorganize your data in many ways if you want to do many different analyses. Using Excel for statistical analysis requires additional attention paid to manipulating rows and columns prior to statistical analysis. But if you are using Excel for simple summaries, simple descriptive tests (correlation, *t* tests, chi-square, and so on), data entry and analysis are appropriate and easily understood and interpretable. Since much of *Schools and Data* deals with simple descriptive statistics, Excel will do just fine.

I include mostly SPSS displays in the text; both Excel and SPSS examples are posted on the Web site at http://www.schoolsand data.org.

A Caution

Statistical programs like SPSS and Excel can handle sophisti-cated data analysis procedures used by any practitioner or gradu-ate student. We must guard against depending on the software to solve our problems, however, especially before we even ask our-selves what is it we want to know from the data. Remember, the essence of using data to improve decision making is not data col-lection or data analysis alone—it is interpretation. And no soft-ware program can make interpretations!

OK, LET'S GIVE IT A GO!

Our first step should first be to organize our data in a comprehen-sible form so that we can spot any trends or patterns that can be seen easily and in turn communicated to our teachers, parents, and students. This is really what we want to accomplish: simplify the organization and presentation of data.

Morris Middle School is a small rural school in central California with an enrollment of 135 students in Grades 5 through 8. The administration for several years has been trying to encour-age teachers at those grade levels to consider collaborative instruc-tional strategies across disciplines. Many of the faculty at Morris Middle School, like many others, feel pretty strongly that "math is math," and "language is language," and never shall the two disci-plines overlap. "After all," they say, "students need separate instruc-tion in these important subjects."

Michael Johnson, the school principal, decides to take a close look at last year's standardized test scores, along with some student demographic data, such as socioeconomic status, gender, ethnicity, and participation in extracurricular activities. Maybe he can orga-nize and present this information to help his teachers understand the relationship between disciplines. For example, one of his hunches is that there might be a relationship between math and language achievement. If so, maybe this information will help the faculty see the connection between instruction and the information we collect and present.

To begin our preliminary analysis of data, let's first create a Morris Middle School data file in SPSS or Excel. You are encouraged to create your own file from scratch (with information about your students) and follow along with the procedures presented in this chapter. It will be easy to follow me using your own students and data. Don't be afraid to use your own variables—you may have interest in collecting additional data (for example, attendance and dropout numbers).

FREQUENCY DISTRIBUTION

One of the common procedures for organizing a set of data is to show it in a *frequency distribution:* an organized tabulation of the number of individuals located in each category on the scale of measurement (Gravetter & Wallnau, 2000). A sample distribution allows the educator to see general trends more easily than does an unordered set of scores. A frequency distribution is a listing, in order of magnitude of each score achieved (or any variable), together with the number of times the score occurred.

We now want to take a close look at some demographic characteristics of our group of middle school students. In other words, what does our group look like? Are the students largely from low socioeconomic backgrounds? Are they predominantly male? Is there a high percentage participating in afterschool activities? To get at the answers to these questions, we must have an understanding of how to obtain and interpret frequency distributions with either SPSS or Microsoft Excel.

Michael first takes a look at the gender and ethnicity of the students at Morris Middle School. Tables 3.1 and 3.2 show the results.

Frequency distributions help us describe the characteristics of the sample or population we are studying. Our sample of students

Table 3.1   Morris Middle School Gender Frequency

Gender	Frequency	Percentage (%)
1 (Male)	75	55.6
2 (Female)	60	44.4
Total	135	100.0

Table 3.2   Morris Middle School Ethnicity Frequency

Ethnicity	Frequency	Percentage (%)
1 (White)	42	31.1
2 (Black)	27	20.0
3 (Hispanic)	66	48.9
Total	135	100.0

is approximately half female and half male, but they represent a variety of cultural and ethnic backgrounds. Will an understanding of these characteristics help us as we design appropriate teaching and learning strategies for Morris School? Let's go on with our analysis and see.

Creating Frequency Distributions With SPSS

With the help of SPSS (or Excel, displayed at: http://www .schoolsanddata.org), creating frequency distributions is easy. From your opening of SPSS, select **New File** or **Type in Data.** From the menu at the top of the screen, select **Analyze**, then **Descriptive Statistics**, then **Frequencies.** A dialogue box appears, allowing you to select the variables on which you want frequency distributions. Click the mouse on the variable you want from the left box, and by clicking the arrow you can move the variable to the right box (a shortcut is to simply double-click the variable, which automatically moves the variable to the right box). Select **OK**, and the frequencies will appear in the output window.

If you want to look at a different frequency distribution, simply return to the dialogue box and repeat the procedure with selecting the desired variables you want displayed in a frequency distribution. Clicking **OK** shows the distribution in the output window in addition to the first frequency. In other words, the output window keeps track of all your frequency reports. When you close the window, SPSS will ask you if you want to save the information in the window. If so, simply select **Save** and give the file a name. This allows you to view or review your frequencies at a later time.

CROSS-TABULATION

The **Frequency** command (as displayed previously in Tables 3.1 and 3.2) can tell us that at Morris Middle School there are 42 White, 27 Black, and 66 Hispanic students (and there are 75 males and 60 females). But it does not show us how many female Hispanic or male Black students we have in our school. SPSS can help us answer those questions with the **Crosstabs** command. **Crosstabs** simply allows us to "cross" two variables (for example, ethnicity and gender). The result is shown in Table 3.3.

Table 3.3   Crosstabs of Gender and Ethnicity

Ethnicity				
Gender	*1 (White)*	*2 (Black)*	*3 (Hispanic)*	*Total*
1 (Male)	27	12	36	75
2 (Female)	15	15	30	60
Total	42	27	66	135

Don't hesitate to try crossing more than two variables (for example, ethnicity, gender, and socioeconomic status). SPSS can handle that easily. After selecting **Crosstabs**, move your desired variables from the list on the left part of the screen to the box on the right (remember the shortcut; double-click on the variable to move to the right box). As stated earlier, statistical analysis does not have to be complicated or complex. However, before we go too much further, we must take a few minutes to discuss *measures of central tendency* and *measures of variability*. This information will help us as we go forward with analyzing various kinds of data found in schools.

MEASURES OF CENTRAL TENDENCY

The most common method for describing and summarizing a set of test scores (or other information expressed as a numerical measure) is to compute the average. You know, for example, "How did our fifth graders do compared to the state average?" In statistics, the concept of averaging is called *central tendency*. Quite simply, the goal of central tendency is to find the average or typical score that provides a reasonably accurate description of the whole class or grade level, for example.

From earlier training in grade school or junior high, we remember that finding the *mean* (the first measure of central tendency) involves adding up all the scores and dividing by the total number of students in the distribution. For example, looking at our Morris Middle School data file, we calculate the mean math score by adding all 135 scores together and then dividing by 135. Wow! Too time consuming, you say? I agree—and too many chances for silly mistakes (error) when adding up all those numbers.

The good news is that we can use our statistical software friends to calculate the mean for us, and we can also ask that the information be added to our printout of information. You probably remember the other two measures of central tendency: the *median* and the *mode*. The median is the score that falls exactly in the middle of the distribution (0.5 if an odd number of scores), and the mode is the most frequently occurring score.

Let's give it a try. Using our Morris Middle School data, ask for a frequency distribution of math scores. Select **Analyze, Descriptive Statistics,** and **Frequencies** using SPSS (**Data Analysis** and **Descriptive Statistics** using Excel). In SPSS, you need to select the measures desired (mean, median, mode) by clicking on the **Statistics** button, then **Continue.** With Excel, simply select **Summary Statistics.** The result will be the three measures of central tendency (mean = 27.16; median = 27; mode = 22) as shown in Table 3.4. Hmmm . . . the mean and median are almost the same—interesting!

Table 3.4   Measures of Central Tendency

N	135
Mean	27.16
Median	27.00
Mode	22

A Caution in Interpretation

Continuing to use our Morris Middle School math scores as an example, we are temped to feel pretty good about our students and their mean score of 27—on our standardized test, a 27 is a respectable achievement score. But we need to be careful about assuming that the whole class did well on their math assessment. Look closely at Table 3.5 and the frequency distribution in relationship to the mean of 27.

Table 3.5   Frequency Distribution

Math Score	Frequency
20	6
21	12
22	15
23	6
24	12
25	12
26	3
27	9
28	12
29	9
30	6
31	3
33	3
34	15
35	3
36	3
37	3
38	3

Yes, we can feel pleased that 69 of our students scored at or above the average of 27. But there is serious cause for alarm when we notice that a similar number (66) of our students scored below the average of 27, with specifically 33 at the very bottom of our distribution. These 33 students didn't seem to affect the mean that much because there was a corresponding number of 27 students who scored very high on our distribution (34–38). Now, data-driven decision making must kick in. What can we do about these 33 students? Could any instructional decisions help raise their scores? Are they perhaps limited-English-speaking students who need additional help in the area of language?

The problem with using the mean to fully describe our group is that the measure does not take into account the spread or range of scores. It does not tell us how our scores are spread out from the mean or how tightly they are centered on the mean. Remember, the calculation of the mean is an *average*. Would it help us to know the mean along with some other measure of spread or variability? Yes, and probably the most important measure to take into consideration when looking at student achievement is the *standard deviation*.

A Frequency Table With Excel

Let's begin with a simple "categorical" frequency distribution using Excel. Posted on the Web site are examples of the other procedures discussed in this chapter. For example, take a small data set of 20 students' math grades: A, B, B, A, B, C, A, A, B, C, C, A, B, A, B, B, C, A, C, B.

1. Select cell A1 and type in all 20 students' grades down Column A of your Excel worksheet.

2. Type in the name **Grades** in cell B1.

3. Select cell B2 and type in the three different grades (A, B, C) down the column.

4. Type in the name **Count** in cell C1.

5. Select cell C2. From the toolbar, select the paste function (*fx*) option. Select **Statistical** from the Function category list. Select **COUNTIFALL** from the function name list.

6. In the dialogue box, type in **A1:A20** in the Range (or simply use your mouse and select cells A1 through A20—this automatically inserts the desired range).

7. For Criteria, type in **A**—click **OK**, and the total number of A's will enter the cell. Repeat this step for the B's and C's.

8. After all the grades have been counted, select cell C5 from the worksheet.

9. From the toolbar, select the *fx* function and choose **Sum**. Then type in **C2:C4** and click **Enter**.

Note: This procedure is posted on the *Schools and Data* Web site under Chapter 3.

MEASURES OF VARIABILITY

Measures of variability provide quantitative measures of the degree to which the scores are spread out or clustered together. With our math scores at Morris Middle School, knowing the mean of 27 is important. But would we not also like to know how many low scores and high scores are present? And *how* high and *how* low? Though there are several measures of variability (range, interquartile range, variance, standard deviation), the standard deviation is the most commonly used and most important measure of variability.

The standard deviation uses the mean as a reference point and measures variability by considering the distance between each score and the mean. Simply, it is an approximate average of all the individual differences between each score and the mean. It is beyond the scope of this book to present or discuss the equations for calculating the standard deviation. Remember, our statistical software packages can do it for us. However, it is important to understand the standard deviation conceptually.

Perhaps an illustration is in order. Think of the standard deviation as a number that helps us describe the middle 68%, representing 1 unit above and 1 unit below the mean (these are called "Z scores," but that is not necessary to know now). Let's return to our Morris Middle School math scores and ask SPSS to calculate a standard deviation (Excel procedures are posted on the Web site at: http://

www.schoolsanddata.org). With SPSS, after selecting **Frequency Distribution**, we select **Statistics** and place a check mark on **standard deviation** (same place we checked mean, median, mode). With Excel, the standard deviation is included when selecting **Summary Statistics.** Now, our report includes a standard deviation of 5 (actually 5.069) along with the frequency distribution. Table 3.6 helps illustrate the additional information we now have regarding our middle school math scores. Subtracting the standard deviation of 5 from our mean gives us 22, and adding 5 to our mean gives us 32—the spread of 68% of our student scores.

Let's suppose for a moment that the standard deviation was 12. The majority (68%) of our student scores would then range from 15 to 39. Wow! The scores are really spread out all over the place. As another example, let's suppose the standard deviation was 2. The majority of our student scores would then range from 25 to 29. Now that's a different story. Most of our students scored very close to the mean of 27 and are stacked or centered very close to the mean.

With our knowledge of measures of central tendency and variability, we can move on to looking at more school data and learning how to make wise data-driven decisions about student achievement. In the following chapters, we begin to look at more strategies to help us describe and explain the data we have in our schools. We also begin to answer some of the questions Michael Johnson asked in the beginning of this chapter: Is there perhaps a relationship between student test scores and socioeconomic status? Is there possibly a relationship between how students perform in math and how they perform in language? Can the data analysis help convince our teachers to do more collaborative teaching across grade levels and subject areas? In Chapter 4, we discuss one of the most common procedures that educators can use to interpret school data. The procedure, called *correlation*, can help us as we make decisions about appropriate and effective instructional strategies.

Simulations, Demonstrations, Interactions

Visit the Web site at: http://www.schoolsanddata.org and view dynamic demonstrations (movies) of the SPSS and Excel procedures covered in this chapter. In addition, a PowerPoint presentation covering the important concepts of the chapter is available for your use. If you have questions after your practice, please use the "Communicate With the Author" link on the Web site's Home Page.

Table 3.6   Morris Students' Math Achievement, Showing Standard
Deviation (Bracketed)

Math Score	Frequency
20	6
21	12
22	15
23	6
24	12
25	12
26	3
27 Mean	9
28	12
29	9
30	6
31	3
32	0
33	3
34	15
35	3
36	3
37	3
38	3

NOTE: One standard deviation above and below the mean equals approximately 68% of the scores (between 22 and 32).

CONCLUSION

Doesn't it seem that we always hear the term *average*? We talk about the "average student," the "average teacher's salary," and even the "average Joe." A measure of central tendency is the most common and most descriptive statistic we use. Generally, it is the single most important description of a sample, a population, or distribution.

The *mean* is the most widely used measure both in our everyday communication and in serious research studies. The mean is the preferred choice because it is affected by each individual score or number. The *median* simply is the 50th percentile of the distribution and is the exact midpoint of the total number of scores. As you can conclude, the disadvantage of the median as a descriptive measure is that it does not reflect an extreme score such as a perfect score on a test or that one "million-dollar home." The *mode* is the most frequently occurring score or number in the distribution and it is not especially valuable to know or as reliable as the mean and median.

As measures of central tendency describe the average or most representative score in the distribution, measures of variability get at the issue of the magnitude of the differences among the scores. In other words, how spread out or how close together are the individual scores? You can imagine the importance of knowing whether a class of math scores ranges from 15 to 99 or from 65 to 99. Though there are several measures of variability, the range, variance, and standard deviation are the most common and valuable. And of these three, the standard deviation is the most important to us in our work in schools. I hope that you now see the importance of both measures of central tendency and variability.

APPLICATION ACTIVITIES

1. Would there ever be a situation in which all three measures of central tendency in a distribution of student test scores would be the same number? Why or why not? If so, what would you say about the group of students with regard to their performance?

2. The mean salary for teachers in Texas is $35,000, and the median salary is $29,000. Draw a distribution curve representing the state's teachers, and comment on why the median salary is lower than the mean salary.

NCLB ACTIVITY

Several congressional hearings during summer 2005 focused on the importance of and strategies for high school reform. In May 2005, the House Committee on Education and the Workforce held a hearing on *High School Reform: Examining State and Local Efforts.* Governor Mitt Romney (R-MA) addressed the committee with the following:

> The attention that we have given to K–8 education over the last few years, and the attention that is now being given to early-childhood education, provides the foundation for our high school and higher education systems. Now, however, it is time to turn focused attention on high school reform—and ensure that the pipeline of students going from high schools into our colleges and universities are ready to compete on a world stage. (Terozzi, 2005, pp. 1–2)

Using what you know about frequency distributions and measures of central tendency and variability, how might you use these tools as you address high school reform based on what we know about school improvement at the elementary and middle school levels?

CHAPTER FOUR

Correlation

My GRE Score Is Not
Good Enough for Harvard!

They told me that my Graduate Record Examination (GRE) scores were not high enough to apply to Harvard (let me pretend for a moment). The Harvard admission folks say they only take graduate students with GRE scores of 1200 and higher (1600 is perfect). Seems they have evidence that students with lower scores have a tendency "not to cut it" and to drop out at a higher rate than those with high GRE scores. They also have evidence that students with 1200 and above have a tendency to do well at Harvard. Sound familiar? (I seem to recall something like this and the Scholastic Aptitude Test—SAT—when I applied to undergraduate schools.)

Much of what we do as educators involves asking questions about two variables. Do students participating in extracurricular activities tend to perform better academically? Do boys tend to excel more than girls in math and computer applications (as we are led to believe), and/or do girls perform better in English and writing? Is there a relationship between grade point averages (GPAs) and success in college? All these questions can be investigated (and maybe answered) using a statistical technique called *correlation*. Quite simply, correlation is used to measure and describe a relationship between two (or more) variables.

Another Caution

There always seems to be a caution, huh? When finding correlations between variables (for example, gender and subject), we must guard against making the assumption that there is a *cause and effect*. In other words, just because there is a strong correlation between X and Y, we cannot assume that X causes an effect on Y or that Y causes an effect on X. Yes, it is important and significant to find whether a correlation exists, but that may only identify a pattern or warrant further investigation. Here's a rather simplistic but obvious example.

When studying the number of drownings on the beaches in California, researchers have found a high correlation between water temperature and number of drownings in the ocean. Figure 4.1 displays the correlation.

Figure 4.1 Relationship Between Drownings and Water Temperature

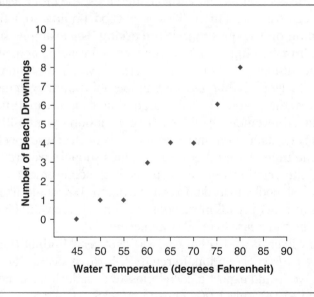

As the temperature of the ocean water increases, so does the number of drownings. This illustrates a *positive correlation*. As one variable increases, so does the other—maybe not in equal increments, but they both have a tendency to move in the same direction. In

addition, as the temperature decreases, so does the number of drownings. Yes, the problem here is fairly obvious—other conditions are at play as well. The caution is to guard against assuming that one variable has a cause/effect on the other. It would be silly to assume that it is the warm water that *causes* the drownings to occur. There are obviously some other variables to consider. Summer means more swimmers (and surfers) on the beaches and more swimmers in the water. A correlation may reveal that a strong *relationship* exists between two variables, but it does not report or even suggest that one *causes* the other to occur. But again, the correlation is extremely important to know—because we can look further to investigate the reasons why.

When we discuss the extent to which variables are related, we use a statistic called *Pearson correlation coefficient*. This coefficient (number) varies between −1.00 and +1.00. Each of these coefficients represents a perfect correlation between the variables: a −1.00 means that as one variable increases, the other decreases, or a negative correlation. This is a good finding sometimes— depending on the question we are asking. For example, suppose we are investigating a relationship between reading achievement and the number of hours of television watched at home. We would likely find that as the number of hours watching TV increases, there would be a corresponding decrease in a student's reading achievement. And a +1.00 correlation (or a positive correlation) exists if both variables increase or decrease together at the same time. As another example, let's suppose we are investigating the relationship between reading achievement and the number of books a student reads at home. We would likely find that as a student reads more books at home, there would be a corresponding increase in reading achievement.

How likely is a +1.00 or a −1.00? Not very! Both of these represent a *perfect* correlation. In reality, this rarely occurs. So, realistically, we would expect a correlation to be a decimal somewhere between +1.00 and −1.00 (for example, .35, .10, −.15, −.45).

Time Out for Some Statistical Jargon

The technical name for the Pearson correlation is the *Pearson product-moment correlation coefficient.* Where did the name come from? In statistics, the deviations about the mean are called *moments,* and if you multiply two moments together, you get the *product* of moments. If you were a statistician named Karl Pearson and you created a way to measure the correlation between two variables, might you call the procedure the Pearson product-moment correlation? The statistical symbol is the lowercase letter *r*, so we shorten the name to *Pearson r*. Not important now, but a heads up: later I will discuss another symbol, r^2, which simply is the coefficient *r squared*. So if our correlation is .20, *r squared* would be .04 (.20 multiplied by .20). Yikes, this is getting too technical. Stay with me, one more item to include here.

Along with the Pearson coefficient, the reporting of *alpha* is critical to whether or not the outcome is *significant*. The *alpha level* or *level of significance* is a probability value (*p*) that is used to determine whether our outcome is significant or not. So, when looking at correlation coefficients, we want to *always* look at the accompanying *level of significance*. We agree in education to set the alpha criteria at .05, so we need a result of $p < .05$ to be considered a significant correlation. Now, here's where it gets a little tricky. As a sample size gets smaller, the magnitude of the correlation must be larger to meet significance, and conversely, as the sample gets larger, the magnitude needed can be smaller to meet significance. Think of it this way: with a small sample, it is easier to get a significant correlation just by chance (get it, change of error and making an incorrect decision). But, the larger the sample, the less chance there is of getting a good correlation just by chance (ah! More power and chance of a correct decision). Whew! Trust me, this will make better sense as we move along.

Back to Our Discussion

Colleges and universities require incoming high school seniors to take either the SAT or the American College Test (ACT) because a positive correlation exists between high SAT or ACT scores and students' academic success at the university. You may ask, "How positive?" Well, certainly not a perfect +1.00 correlation. That would mean there were no exceptions, and all college students had high SAT or ACT scores (and to the same degree). I, along with several of you, would like to question such a correlation. In actuality, the correlation is approximately +.35, meaning the relationship is positive (direction) and pretty strong (strength).

Interestingly, a correlation only tells us two things for sure: (1) the direction of the relationship (positive or negative) and (2) the strength of the relationship (0 to + or −1.00). Yes, even if the correlation is 0, that is an important finding—meaning that there is no relationship at all. Again, based on the research question, we might want to find no relationship. For example, let's suppose we are investigating whether or not there might be a relationship between a student's height and math achievement. Yes, maybe another simplistic example, but we would hope there is no relationship between these two variables ($r = 0.00$).

A negative (−) correlation exists if students who score low on one variable tend to score high on a second variable and if students score high on the first variable tend to score low on the second variable. A good example is the fact that sometimes students who score very high in math and science tend to score lower in English and language arts. Here at the university, we struggle with the evidence that suggests a negative correlation between the athletic ability of athletes and their grade point average—such that as the athlete's ability increases, his or her grade point average tends to decrease. Again, not a perfect negative correlation (−1.00), but strong enough to cause coaches and college presidents concern. The current solution, though not very successful, is to provide tutors for the athletes. You can guess a problem with this solution. What about tutors for nonathletes who may have other kinds of deficiencies, such as limited English skills, or who come from environments of poverty? Do we offer them the same treatment? Most of the faculty and student body believe not and feel that this perhaps borders on preferential treatment for the athletes.

I think it is helpful to repeat that correlation only measures two things: (1) strength (reported by a decimal) and (2) direction (negative indicated by the minus sign). For instance, a correlation of .95 means a very strong relationship (almost a perfect 1.00) in a positive direction. A correlation coefficient of −.95 means a very strong relationship (almost a perfect −1.00) in a negative direction. Figure 4.2 displays a series of scatter diagrams illustrating a variety of correlations (relationships) between two variables.

As you notice, the greater the tendency for the student scores to fall on a straight line, the closer the scores are to a perfect correlation (+1.00 or −1.00). If no pattern or linear relationship exists, the correlation approximates 0.00.

Figure 4.2   Relationship or Correlation Between Two Variables

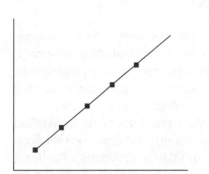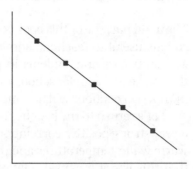

Pearson *r* = + 1.00 (perfect positive)   Pearson *r* = – 1.00 (perfect negative)

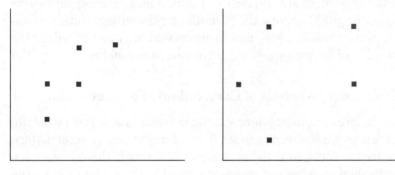

Pearson *r* = 0.08   Pearson *r* = 0.06

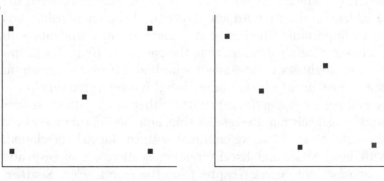

Pearson *r* = – 0.00   Pearson *r* = – 0.40

WHY WOULD EDUCATORS BE INTERESTED IN CORRELATIONS?

The main purpose of this book is to present statistical tools and applications useful to teachers, administrators, central office personnel, and professors and students in principal preparation programs as they make decisions for school improvement. So get to it, you say! Tell me how correlations will help me in my daily life as an educator.

Let's return to the beaches of California for a moment. We find a very strong positive correlation (strength and direction) between warm water temperatures and the number of drownings. Realizing that this is not a causal relationship, we can perhaps predict an increase in drownings in June, July, and August, when water temperatures are higher. Therefore, we would be wise to double the number of lifeguards on duty or position lifeguards on surfboards to better guard against the potential for drowning. In this example, the correlation was used to *predict* and, we hope, to reduce the number of drownings—data-driven decision making.

Preliminary Analysis of Correlations: The Scatterplot

Before conducting any specific correlations, it is very helpful to first plot a scatterplot to see if there might be a general pattern or trend. You know, the scatterplot is a graph that shows each individual member's score on one variable against his or her score on the second variable. Scatterplots can tell us much by a single glance: (1) whether or not there is any relationship between the variables, (2) the strength and direction of the relationship, and (3) as important, whether or not there are any students with scores significantly different than the pattern or trend. For example, you might spot one student who had a perfect score on an exam, or a student who for some strange reason scored very low—we call such cases *outliers.* You see, either one of these outliers would drastically bias the relationship, and this information would be helpful to us before we continue with the formal correlation. With both SPSS and Excel, creating scatterplots is easy and straightforward. Select **Graphs** from the menu, select **Scatter,** and then select or define the variables you wish to plot. If you need help, visit http://www.schoolsanddata.org, where I have posted the scatterplot procedure for both SPSS and Excel in the simulations/demonstrations.

A SCHOOL MUSIC PROGRAM: A CASE STUDY

Bob, an elementary and junior high school music teacher, works in a district that makes a strong commitment to music and the arts in its curriculum. The community is as proud of its music program as it is of its athletic teams. It is not surprising that Bob is expected to have a nationally recognized junior high school band and orchestra. The community and central office have a long tradition of support (both financial and otherwise) for their music program. Because Bob is also the music teacher for the two elementary schools feeding into the junior high school, he has the opportunity to train excellent elementary students in the beginning band and orchestra who will later move into his nationally recognized junior high band and orchestra.

Bob's ongoing effort, and what keeps him awake some nights, is recruiting. How can he effectively recruit quality musicians for his junior high program? How can he *predict* that the students he selects at the elementary level will mature and develop into the excellent musicians required in his junior high school performing groups? His hunch or *research question* is, "Is there a relationship between students' academic performance and their performance or success in music?" Though he realizes that there are exceptions to this rule, he still believes there might be something to his hunch.

Bob decides to investigate any relationship between students' success in music and their disaggregated state standardized test scores. In other words, he suspects that there may be a relationship between certain academic areas (for example, reading, math science, social studies) and musical ability. Maybe students who are good readers learn to read music better and faster. Maybe students who work well in science lab groups together possess the collaborative skills necessary to perform musically with others.

He collects the final music grades from his past 4 years of junior high school music students, transforming letter grades to grade point equivalents. Table 4.1 displays his grade transformation strategy.

Bob then wants to see if a relationship exists between music performance grades and students' individual Iowa Test of Basic Skills (ITBS) scores. The answers to his questions might help with his recruiting and selecting at the elementary level. He reasons that if a high number of students who perform at a high level in

Table 4.1   Music Grade Transformation Scale

Grade	GPA
A+	4.5
A	4.0
A−/B+	3.5
B	3.0
B−/C+	2.5
C	2.0
C−	1.5
D/F	1.0

music also share a characteristic of high science scores, there will be a positive correlation between the two. And if so, he will consider using science scores at the elementary level as a predictor of future success in his junior high school band and orchestra. Table 4.2 displays a small sample of *hypothetical* data and how this correlation might look if Bob's hypothesis were correct.

First, you notice that there is a pattern of both variables moving in the same direction. The student with a music GPA of 2.5 scored 180 on the science assessment and the student with a music GPA of 3.0 scored 190 on the science assessment. Looking further

Table 4.2   Relationship Between Music Grades and ITBS Science Test Scores (Hypothetical)

Music Student Number	Music Grades	Science Scores
1	2.5	180
2	4.0	210
3	3.5	200
4	4.5	220
5	3.0	190

at each of the higher GPAs, we see a corresponding increase in science scores. We know that the correlation is going to be positive (direction) because both variables are moving in the same increasing manner. Do we know how strong the relationship is? Not exactly—but let's look closer. Remember, a perfect correlation could exist if the increases were incremental and increased the same amount between each of the five GPAs. Sure enough, each increase of 0.5 in GPA equals a science score increase of 10 points. Can you guess what the correlation coefficient is in this example? Yes, a perfect correlation of +1.00. As one variable increases, the other variable increases by an equal amount. How likely is this to occur in real life? Not very. Though this example is not realistic, I hope it helped to conceptualize the correlation procedure. Now, let's go back to Bob and his real-life dilemma.

SPSS and Excel—Help!

Before we rush into correlations on the computer, allow me to digress for a moment. Yes, there is a formula for calculating correlation coefficients by hand. As has been the practice in this book, I do not emphasize or encourage the use of formulas for calculation. With your permission, however, allow me to touch on the issue lightly. As much as I encourage the early use of computer software for statistical analysis, there is a caution (here he goes again—another caution). Sometimes it is detrimental to rush into computer analysis, especially if you are having difficulty with the conceptual understanding of the procedure. In those cases, it can be helpful to calculate a small sample by hand to get the basic understanding of the process. As promised, I will not elaborate on complex formulas and calculations—the calculation of the Pearson notwithstanding. However, you might want to consult a formal statistics text and review the hand calculation of the Pearson *r*, using the *raw score method*. It is actually pretty straightforward, using nothing more than squaring, summing, cross products, and the square root.

OK, enough of that. Using data from Resource A, create a file titled, "Music Correlation." You will notice Bob's sample of 24 music students, their music grades, and their sets of scores for math, language, and science. Remember Bob's research question: Is there perhaps a correlation or relationship between students' music performance and their academic performance? And if so, can he use the information to help him recruit and select music students at the elementary level for his junior high band and orchestra program?

Microsoft Excel

Enter the data from Resource A in a new Excel worksheet. Renumber the individual students in Column A, band grades in Column B, and math, language, and science scores in Columns C, D, and E respectively, as shown in Figure 4.3.

Figure 4.3   Excel Data Input

	A	B	C	D	E	F	G	H
1	Student	Band	Math	Language	Science			
2	1	3	220	215	220			
3	2	4	240	210	225			
4	3	2.5	210	250	235			
5	4	2	215	230	210			
6	5	4	260	240	220			
7	6	3	230	270	250			
8	7	3.5	240	240	220			
9	8	4	259	220	240			
10	9	3	245	230	250			
11	10	4	280	270	230			
12	11	4.5	300	260	220			
13	12	2	230	250	225			
14	13	3	250	245	235			
15	14	4	275	235	210			
16	15	2.5	200	260	220			
17	16	2	200	255	250			
18	17	4	290	250	220			
19	18	3	250	230	240			
20	19	3.5	270	245	250			
21	20	4	280	270	230			
22	21	3	260	270	260			
23	22	4	270	250	230			
24	23	4.5	310	260	280			
25	24	2	170	250	220			

From the Excel menu, select **Tools > Data Analysis > Correlation.** Click the icon next to the **Input Range** box. This will minimize the dialogue box. Use the mouse to highlight the data from Columns B, C, D, and E. Once the data are selected, click the icon to restore the box. Make sure that the data are grouped by columns, and select **New Worksheet Ply**, then click **OK**. The result is Figure 4.4.

Figure 4.4 Excel Correlation Matrix

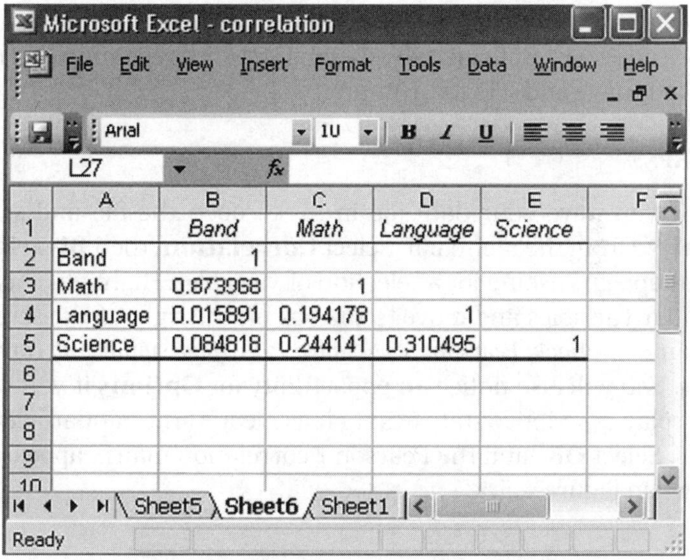

	A	B	C	D	E	F
1		*Band*	*Math*	*Language*	*Science*	
2	Band	1				
3	Math	0.873968	1			
4	Language	0.015891	0.194178	1		
5	Science	0.084818	0.244141	0.310495	1	

You should first realize that the cells with a correlation coefficient of 1.00 are at points where each variable meets with itself. For example, in cell B2, Band Grades is correlated with itself, Band Grades—and is a positive 1.00. This information is of no interest to us—the other cells hold the information we are after.

Now, let's see what the matrix reveals. Bob is interested in three pieces of information: (1) the relationship between music and math, .873; (2) the relationship between music and language, .015; and (3) the relationship between music and science, .084. First of all, the relationship (correlation) between music and language and music and science is positive, but very low and almost nonexistent. Remember, as the coefficient approximates zero, it reveals less and less correlation or relationship.

The matrix reveals a correlation of .873 between music grades and math scores. This correlation is positive and quite strong. As the coefficient approximates 1.00, it reveals more and more relationship between the variables. If we check a Pearson critical value table, from any statistics book, we find that with a sample of 135 and at an alpha level of .05, we only need a coefficient of .20 to be considered significant. *Wow!* The music grades/math correlation is so strong that it really meets the criteria for an alpha level (*p*) of .01. Our selected alpha level is usually .05, but in this case the correlation meets the more stringent .01 level. Bob's discovery is that a strong correlation exists between math and music grades, but a rather insignificant correlation exists between music grades and language and science. Hmmm . . . !

SPSS

If you have your data file in SPSS, open the file and select **Analyze** from the menu bar. Select **Correlation,** then **Bivariate.** A box appears asking for a selection of variables. Highlight each of the four variables and move to the box on the right of the screen. Be sure to check *Pearson, Two-Tailed,* and *flag significant correlations.* You will also notice an opportunity for **Options** if you wish to display descriptive statistics such as means and standard deviations. Select **OK,** and the Pearson *r* correlation matrix appears as shown in Figure 4.5.

So What Does This Mean for Bob?

First, in SPSS, significant correlations are flagged with one star if meeting the .05 criteria and two stars if a stronger correlation exists, meeting the more stringent .01 alpha level. We see here two stars between math grades and music grades. Remembering the caution issued earlier to guard against assuming cause and effect with correlations, we note that Bob's analysis does not prove that students who receive high grades in math also develop into exemplary musicians. However, there is sufficient reason to believe that for some reason (unknown at this point) there is a relationship between math and music achievement. We might conjecture that music possesses mathematical components (actually, it does) and students who are good in math may progress in music faster and with greater success. I assume Bob will look more closely at the relationship and probably will use this correlation result in his recruiting plans at the elementary level.

Figure 4.5   SPSS Correlation Matrix

		Band	Math	Language	Science
Band	Pearson Correlation	1	.874(**)	.016	.085
	Sig. (2-tailed)		.000	.941	.694
	N	24	24	24	24
Math	Pearson Correlation	.874(**)	1	.194	.244
	Sig. (2-tailed)	.000		.363	.250
	N	24	24	24	24
Language	Pearson Correlation	.016	.194	1	.310
	Sig. (2-tailed)	.941	.363		.140
	N	24	24	24	24
Science	Pearson Correlation	.085	.244	.310	1
	Sig. (2-tailed)	.694	.250	.140	
	N	24	24	24	24

OTHER DATA-DRIVEN DECISION MAKING

Though Bob was not interested in looking at the relationships of the other variables with each other, the analysis reveals something of interest to us. What were the correlations among the three subjects? Not so significant. In other words, students who were receiving high grades in math were not really achieving high grades in language and science. This is somewhat troubling, for we know from previous studies that, in general, high-achieving students in one subject area tend to also do well in others. Not a perfect correlation, but pretty strong and positive.

As Bob's principal, I would want to investigate further or conduct further studies in an attempt to discover why those students' language and science scores were noticeably lower. However, Bob might argue (and with justification) that this finding just points to the relationship between performance in music and high achievement in mathematics. Again, the Pearson r does not reveal reasons for the correlation, but there is certainly a reason for concern.

I think my first step would be to talk with the teachers of the students in question to get another assessment of their performance in language and science. Perhaps their actual performance is different than the results of our standardized test. A couple other questions come to mind: Can we really assess language skills so easily on a standardized test? Can we really assess science skills on a standardized test? Maybe our assessment procedures in language and science should include more performance-based strategies.

A common result in statistical analysis: more questions have been raised than answered. However, this is not cause for despair but cause for celebration. We as educators need to harness some of the power and potential of data analysis with regard to decision making at the school site.

The Spearman Correlation

Again, without getting too technical, I will touch lightly on the Spearman correlation, which is used within SPSS in a different situation. The Spearman correlation measures the relationship between variables that are placed on an *ordinal* or *categorical scale* of measurement. Sometimes we have data that are in rank order. For instance, the cafeteria cooks are interested in students' preference for different menu items. Five meals are presented in survey form, and students respond with answers of first, second, third, fourth, and fifth. If we were to conduct a correlation study with menu preference, we would use the Spearman method. On the other hand, we sometimes have *categorical* data—you know, Republicans, Democrats, and Independents. Again, with these data, we would use the Spearman correlation. Good news—you only need to know that when running the tests in SPSS, simply check **Spearman** instead of **Pearson**. That's it for Spearman—all examples in *Schools and Data* use the Pearson correlation.

CONCLUSION

In my experience as a teacher, principal, and superintendent, and now university professor, the majority of questions and concerns I have had over the years have really been correlational. Most questions related to teaching and learning involve the degree to which two variables go together. If we can identify the variable or variables that influence a certain behavior, there is a tremendous potential for helping students become successful. If there were only one statistical tool that I could pass on to you, it would be correlation. Let me close this chapter on correlation with a study conducted at an area school district a few years ago.

Collaborative Teaching and Integrated Curriculum

I was approached by a local school superintendent. Sarah was concerned about the lack of collaborative instructional activities at her high school. As is common in many high schools, often our curriculum is so compartmentalized we create learning environments boxed in by four walls. The box is math, this other box is English, and this one here is just for science. You know, you have been there. Teachers can become very territorial and specialized in such an environment.

Sarah's desire was to help her faculty realize the interconnectedness of different subject areas. She was aware of much of the research indicating that students can learn math in the gymnasium. Language skills are also encouraged in science classes. The evidence goes on and on. Sarah began by asking if we could look at her school's data in an effort to improve her wish for a more integrated curriculum at this high school.

In looking at the high school's standardized and performance-based assessment data, we discovered what Sarah suspected— there was a very high correlation between the individual course results and student achievement. The relationships between achievement in one course and achievement in others were pretty strong and positive. In other words, students who did well in English also had a tendency to do well in math, science, and other courses. This was not earth shattering to discover, but it caused Sarah to begin thinking and asking the following questions:

If I can show my faculty the strong correlation between students' achievement scores across the various subject areas, might it help them realize the interconnectedness of all learning? Maybe we can talk about how our math teachers and English teachers can develop collaborative activities that would benefit both subject areas at the same time. Doesn't it make sense to blend science and math together when the two courses use so many similar skills? Shouldn't our music teachers have a shared understanding of math, science, and language skills?

Sarah's plan moved forward. Her objective progressed to the point that her faculty began to agree that perhaps this thing called *correlation* had some benefit as they struggled to improve their curriculum and develop a more collaborative teaching and learning environment at the high school.

As always seems to happen, data analysis posed more questions to ponder. In the process of looking at correlations, the faculty even noticed some significant findings related to gender. They were encouraged to find out that there was no significant correlation between math achievement and gender. In other words, girls were achieving just as consistently as boys in math and were equally represented in the advanced math classes such as trigonometry and calculus.

However, one finding surfaced that concerned both the administration and teachers. There seemed to be a significant correlation between English composition assessment and gender. A great number of girls were receiving the higher grades, and in general boys were not performing as well. Again, maybe this is not an earth-shattering finding, but this particular group of faculty and administration were deeply troubled and decided they were not satisfied with this result.

At the end of a workshop with the faculty, I was approached by the high school principal. He reluctantly offered his solution to the problem of composition and gender, stating that he did not feel comfortable offering his remarks to the entire faculty. His theory (or hypothesis) was that for years, all the high school composition teachers had been female and had had a tendency to assign topics for writing that were of more interest to girls than boys. He was not meaning to appear "sexist" with his comment; rather, he was suggesting that there might be a correlation between assigned topics in composition and student achievement.

The end of the story is a happy one. The principal eventually presented his hypothesis to his three English composition faculty, and to his surprise, they agreed that perhaps the assignments in the class needed to be reviewed. Again, proof? No, but a pattern uncovered by a correlation study presented an opportunity for some real data-driven decision making. The result was two decisions:

(1) more thought would go into the choice of composition assignments, offering a wider variety of topic choices, and (2) the composition and science faculty developed and implemented several collaborative activities that had students using writing skills in science but also encouraged students to suggest science-related topics in composition class.

APPLICATION ACTIVITIES

1. Create a file using the math and language scores for a small group of students at your school. Conduct a Pearson correlation between student math and language test scores. The question is, What is the relationship between math and verbal skills or achievement? What does the test reveal, and what might be some of the instructional reasons for the outcome of this particular group of students?

2. Select 20 students from your school. Create an SPSS or Excel data file that includes the students' standardized test scores for science and math. One of your questions is, Do students who receive high test scores in math also have a tendency to receive high test scores in science? Disaggregate the data by breaking them down into two groups, male and female. When you run separate correlations on males and females, are there noticeable patterns of differences in strength and direction of correlation coefficients?

NCLB ACTIVITY

One of the No Child Left Behind (NCLB) legislation requirements states that "verification of each state's assessment system via required participation (every other year) by selected districts will be conducted with the National Assessment of Educational Progress (NAEP)." Suppose you are interested in investigating whether or not your students' state assessment scores are correlated with their NAEP scores. In other words, just because your students may do well on state tests does not mean their national performance might correspond. And if not, what steps might you take to increase the correlation in a stronger positive direction? On the other hand, if there exists a strong correlation, how would you interpret that result?

CHAPTER FIVE

Introduction to Regression

In the previous chapter, we learned the usefulness of correlation. One of the frustrations of each statistical procedure is the realization of its limitations—seems like we always come up against the following: "This works well for this, but by the way, we need to use something else to really get at what we want to investigate." In our desire to have immediate answers and find a procedure that does it all, this is truly frustrating. But, just realize that statistics is only a set of tools, and like traditional tools, the hammer pounds nails pretty well, but it does not cut a 2-by-4; so we use a saw for that purpose. And if we decide we want to put some holes in the 2-by-4—yikes! Neither tool will work—we need a new tool called a drill. Simplistic analogy perhaps—but really the same dilemma we face with using statistics to help with decision making about school improvement. We need a whole tool kit of procedures.

So yes, correlation has some limitations and, in a sense, an absence of power. We begin now to talk about power—meaning, How confident are we about a certain decision, once we analyze the data? For example, how powerful is the decision to use whole language strategies in fourth grade reading based on a study comparing whole language with the phonics approach? If there is an absence of power, we run the risk of making an incorrect decision. If there is power, we can be more confident that we are making a wise and appropriate decision.

You may recall me saying, "Correlation only measures two things: (1) relationship and (2) direction." It can reveal important patterns in test scores, for example, but I might have further interest in trying to predict one variable based on the other. I want to know if I can predict student success based on the time spent studying in the library. Correlation can be a very useful tool, but it tells us nothing about the predictive power of variables (Field, 2005). Bob, our junior high music teacher in Chapter 4, may not have been aware of it, but he was really interested in *prediction*. He wanted to be able to *predict* student success in his music program.

Think for a moment about the following four questions:

1. Are two or more variables related?

2. If so, what is the strength and direction of the relationship?

3. What type of relationship exists?

4. What kind of predictions can we make from the relationship?

These are really the questions we want answered in our quest for school improvement and increased student achievement, aren't they? If we are investigating the relationship between hours a student studies at home and how well he or she will do on the state assessment, we are asking: (1) Are the two things related, (2) if so, how strong and in what direction is the relationship, (3) what type of relationship exists, and (4) can I predict student success based on how many hours he or she studies at home?

We have already discovered how to answer the first two questions: correlation. To get at the answers to the third and fourth questions, we need a different tool. This tool is called *regression:* a statistical method used to further describe the nature of the relationship between variables. For example, is the relationship *linear* (straight line) or *nonlinear* (curved line)? Hang on, we'll take this slowly.

Before we go any further, we must take a moment to discuss two kinds of regression: *simple* regression and *multiple* regression. Stay with me—I know you already understand this, at least conceptually. Let me return to our interest in student success and hours of study at home. If we find a very strong positive relationship between these two variables (that is, as a student spends more hours of study at home, he or she is very likely to score better on our state assessment exam), we may be able to create a pretty reliable method of prediction. *But,* would you also agree that student success is not based 100% on hours of study at home? What about motivation? What about innate intelligence? What about parents' education level? What about socioeconomic level? You get it—yes, there are many other variables that cause students to learn and achieve.

Back to the third question raised earlier: There are two types of relationship: simple and multiple. In a simple relationship, there are only two variables investigated—say, for example, hours of study and student achievement. This is a simple relationship. If on the other hand, we want to investigate many variables at once, this is a multiple relationship. Now substitute the word *regression* for *relationship*. Get it? Simple regression seeks to predict an outcome from a single predictor, whereas multiple regression seeks to predict an outcome from several predictors.

SIMPLE REGRESSION

To conceptually understand regression, it is helpful if we think of a straight line (linear relationship). Remember in our discussion in Chapter 4 about correlations, we drew straight lines to represent correlations of .50, 1.00, −.33, −1.00, and so on. It is kind of the same thing here—we want to construct a straight line that can be used to predict (regression). This line, by the way, is called a *regression line*. Look at the scatterplot displayed in Figure 5.1.

We see a very positive relationship between math and science scores for this sample of students (statistically, the correlation in this example is $r = .82$). This only means that the relationship is pretty noticeable (strong) and it is in a positive direction (as students score high in math, they also seem to score high in science). Not perfectly, but in a pretty reliable way. *Can you imagine a line drawn to represent this sample?* Yes, we can actually see several lines that might be drawn. Take a look at Figure 5.2.

But, here's the dilemma: Which line would *best fit* the distribution of scores? Hmmm. . . . Here is the technical definition for regression:

> The statistical technique for finding the best-fitting straight line for a set of data is called *regression*, and the resulting straight line is called a *regression line*.

Figure 5.1   Linear Relationship Between Math and Science Scores

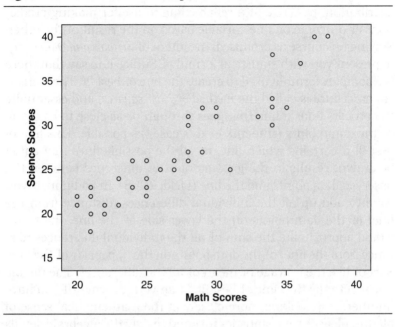

Figure 5.2   Straight Lines Representing Relationship Between Math
and Science Scores

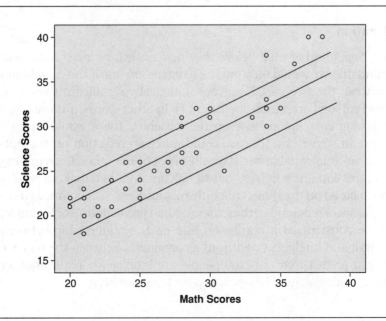

So you see, we need a way to place the line of best fit on our distribution, to arrive at a reliable line to use for making predictions of outcome on one variable based on the result of the other. Staying on course as promised, the intent of *Schools and Data* is not to present you with statistical formulas. Suffice it to say that there is a complex formula used to create the line of best fit. The statistical procedure is called the *method of least squares,* and essentially the process finds a line that goes through or as close to as many of the data points (students in this case) as possible. This line of best fit ascertains which line, of all the possible lines that could be drawn, results in the least amount of difference between the observed data points and the line (Field, 2005). In addition, if you were to add up all the individual differences (distance from the line) of the data points on the lower side of the line, the result would approximate the sum of all the individual differences (distance from the line) of the data points on the upper side of the line. Sort of like the average or mean of all the differences. The middle line is actually the "line of best fit." Can you see why? (If you have an interest in looking more closely at the mathematical sense of all this, please visit a statistics text and review the algebraic details of constructing straight lines—that is, intercepts and slopes.) Whew! Enough of that for now—let's get back to reality!

Caution

Yep, another one! Before moving forward, we need to keep in mind that we would only pursue a regression line if the correlation between the two variables were statistically significant (based on the Pearson correlation coefficient r). In other words, if there is not a strong correlation between the variables, there would be little sense in suggesting that we could make a prediction on the outcome of one variable based on the effect of the other. Determining a regression line when r is not significant and then making predictions based on that line is not only meaningless, it encourages us to make incorrect (and perhaps dangerous) predictions. For example, if we constructed a regression line on the relationship between height and intelligence without a correlation between the two, we might predict that only tall people are intelligent. Yeah, another simplistic analogy—I suspect you see the point here.

Some Basic Steps to Follow in Simple Regression

Even before conducting a correlation between the two variables under investigation, there is a benefit in looking at the simple scatterplot of your data (see Figures 5.1 and 5.2). Let's take a try at another set of variables: the relationship between student achievement and the number of hours a student studies at home. Our research questions might be, (1) Is there a relationship between student achievement and the number of hours studied at home per week? and (2) If there is a significant relationship, can we predict how well students will do academically based on the number of hours studied at home? If so, we have some powerful data to share with our students, administration, and colleagues. Let's use the small data set displayed in Table 5.1.

Table 5.1   GPA and Hours Studied at Home per Week

Student GPA	Number of Hours Studied per Week
3.5	6
2.8	5
3.6	6
2.5	4
2.7	3
3.4	5
3.3	5
3.8	4
3.9	6
2.8	3

Place these data in either SPSS or Excel (both analyses posted on the *Schools and Data* Web site). First, let's ask for a simple scatterplot (Figure 5.3).

Figure 5.3   Grade Point Average Related to Hours of Study per Week

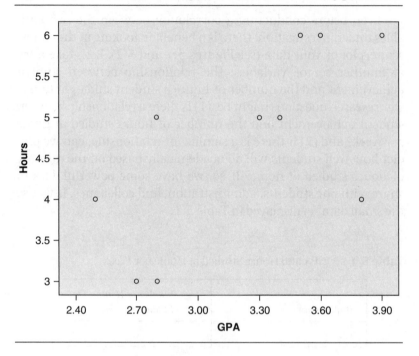

Hmmm . . . What do you think? Any noticeable pattern? Yep, think so. Seems to be a pattern revealing that as hours of study per week increase, so does the grade point average (GPA). We would be shocked if the opposite pattern existed. Can you imagine a *line of best fit?* The bird's-eye view of our data gives us enough initial evidence that perhaps we have a strong positive correlation. Conducting a Pearson correlation reveals: $r = .657$, $p = .039$. That's pretty strong and certainly falls within our criteria of $p < .05$ as our selected alpha level.

A Note About r^2

I mentioned earlier that we have to be careful about assuming cause and effect with a correlation coefficient. In other words, $r = .657$ is strong, but we cannot assume that "hours studied at home" will absolutely 100% of the time cause a student's GPA to increase. However, we can interpret the correlation a step further: if we square the correlation coefficient, we get a measure of the amount of variability in one variable that is explained by the other. Obviously, we both agree that many variables account for whether or not a student's GPA increases. There are such things as motivation, interest in subject, support and expertise of teacher, support from parents, and many others that might cause a student to perform better academically. *The correlation coefficient squared* (r^2) gives us a pretty accurate estimate of the variability that one variable is responsible for. In other words, in our example here, squaring .66 results in approximately .43, or turning it into a percentage, 43% of the variance in GPA is explained by hours of study spent at home. Again, we must be careful in using this to infer causal relationships—though this relationship is very strong, there remains approximately 57% of the variance explained by other variables. Though hours spent studying at home can account for 43% of the variation in GPA (in this sample only), it does not necessarily cause this variation.

So, How Do We Conduct a Simple Regression?

Please trust me that the formulas and technical procedures used for SPSS and Excel are appropriate and accurate in assessing a regression question, and we will not get too technical in our discussion of them. But, in order to make a prediction of how much one variable affects the other, we need to interpret information from a couple of rather complex tables provided by the SPSS regression procedure. I will try to keep it simple and present the procedure in a conceptual way. Let's walk through the steps using our data set of GPA and hours of study at home. Be reminded that the procedures for entering the data in both SPSS and Excel are posted on the schoolsanddata.org Web site.

The data file has two columns: (1) entered in Column 1 are the 10 students' GPAs, and (2) entered in Column 2 are the hours of study at home for each corresponding student. (Always remember to enter your data in different columns for SPSS.)

Before we concern ourselves with either correlation or the regression model, let's view our data on a scatterplot (Figure 5.4). We first notice that the existing relationship is a positive one, with a pattern showing that as the number of hours studied at home increases, so does the student's GPA. Obviously the relationship is not perfect or 1.00—actually there is one student with a high GPA who studies only 4 hours per week (top left) and another student who studies 5 hours per week but has a lower GPA (bottom right). The point is that here again, we have a pattern, and a line of best fit can be drawn to show a fairly good model to use for predicting GPA based on a student's hours of study at home.

Figure 5.4   GPA Scatterplot

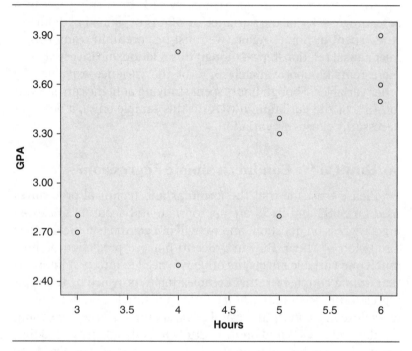

To find the specifics of the line of best fit, and to determine whether this model can help us with our desire to predict a student's GPA, we need to run a simple regression analysis on SPSS or Excel. For this data set, I feature SPSS (also posted on our Web site at: http://www.schoolsanddata.org). To run the analysis, access the dialogue box (as shown in Figure 5.5) by selecting **Analyze** from the menu, then **Regression**, then **Linear.** Place *GPA* in the Dependent box and *hours* in the Independent box—notice that the Independent box allows for more than one entry. We are running a simple regression here—meaning that we only have one predictor variable (hours of study), but if we were running a multiple regression, we would enter more than one variable in that box.

And yes, there are several options available, but we will just run the regression analysis as is.

Figure 5.5   SPSS Regression Box

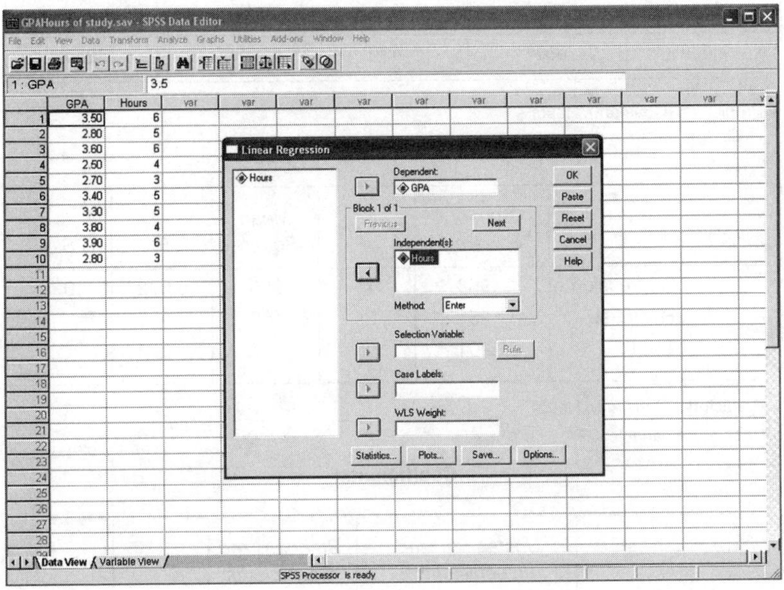

So, How Do We Interpret the Analysis?

After selecting **OK,** we get three output tables from SPSS (see Figure 5.6). Let's interpret the first output table, entitled "Model Summary." We are really interested in the correlation (r) and the r^2. The correlation of our two variables is a positive .657, giving us a pretty good indication that as our predictor variable (hours of study at home) increases, so does our students' GPA. Remember my earlier comments about the value of squaring the correlation coefficient? The r^2 tells us that hours of study at home can account for approximately 43% of the variation of how well a student achieves as measured by GPA. Hmmm . . . ! As important as this sounds, we must be reminded that there is a remaining 57% not accounted for—meaning that approximately 57% of what causes students to have high GPAs comes from *other* variables (for example, intelligence, motivation, desire, resiliency). OK, but still we have some encouraging news here.

Figure 5.6   SPSS Regression Report

Regression

Model Summary

Model	R	Adjusted R Square	Std. Error of R Square	the Estimate
1	.657[a]	.432	.360	.39548

a. Predictors: (Constant), Hours

ANOVA[b]

Model		Sum of Squares	df	Mean Square	F	Sig.
1	Regression	.950	1	.950	6.072	.039[a]
	Residual	1.251	8	.156		
	Total	2.201	9			

a. Predictors: (Constant), Hours
b. Dependent Variable: GPA

Coefficients[a]

Model		Unstandardized Coefficients		Standardized Coefficients	t	Sig.
		B	Std. Error	Beta		
1	(Constant)	1.913	.549		3.486	.008
	Hours	.280	.114	.657	2.464	.039

a. Dependent Variable: GPA

The second table of the SPSS output in Figure 5.6 reports an analysis of variance (ANOVA). Trust me—though we have several numbers here that look confusing and complex, we are at this point only interested in the F value and the Significance in the last two columns on the right side of the table. For our set of data, F is 6.07, which is significant at $p < .05$, meaning that there is less than a 5% chance that an F value this large would occur by chance alone. Good news again! We can conclude that this regression model is a significantly better prediction method than if we used the mean alone. Really, it means that our model is a pretty good predictor of GPA (based on hours of study).

OK so far. The ANOVA table in Figure 5.6 tells us that we have a pretty reliable prediction method, but it does not tell us specifically what degree of GPA might be affected by an additional hour of study or even an extra 30 minutes of study per week. The last table in the SPSS output (Coefficients) gets at some of these specific questions and allows us to really pinpoint the degree to which hours of study can be used to predict a student's GPA. Now, this gets pretty technical, but stay with me—and trust that I am leading you in the right direction.

The third output table in Figure 5.6 (Coefficients) provides some of the specifics we are after. These figures are based on a formula that looks closely at the regression line, its slope, and where it intercepts the Y-axis. From the table, the $B = 1.9$ can be interpreted to mean that if a student does not study at all at home (0 hours), the model predicts a GPA of approximately 1.9. Now, notice the second number under B (.280). Technically, this represents the gradient or slope of the regression line, but we can think of this value as representing the change of the outcome (GPA) based on one unit of change in the predictor (hours of study). In other words, if our predictor is increased by one unit (an hour of study), then our model predicts that a student's GPA would increase by .28. So, using the finding that if a student does not study at all (0 hours), he or she is likely to approximate a GPA of 1.9, we can predict that if a student studies 1 hour a week, his or her GPA might increase to 2.18 (1.9 plus .28). The t values and significances of $p < .05$ confirm the reliability of our regression model. In summary, we can be pretty confident that our model predicts GPA significantly well.

Visit http://www.schoolsanddata.org to view and study the regression procedure using Microsoft Excel.

CONCLUSION

In the previous chapter, we learned that the Pearson correlation is a technique for measuring and describing the linear relationship between two variables, but has limitations in that it only identifies the strength and direction of the relationship. In this chapter, we extended the concept to allow us to make predictions about an outcome of one variable based on the action of another using regression analysis. Important to the procedure of regression is the "line of best fit," not only making the relationship easier to see, but also to serve as a "formula" for calculating the prediction. This line of best fit establishes a precise relationship between each value on the X-axis (hours of study) and a corresponding value on the Y-axis (GPA). So, as in our example in this chapter, we can use the straight line relationship to predict that a student who studies 5 hours per week at home should achieve a GPA of 3.30.

It is beyond the scope of *Schools and Data* to present and discuss the specific formulas used in regression analysis. On the other hand, the intent is to give an understanding of the concept and a working knowledge of the process. The author strongly recommends that once school leaders see the purpose, goal, and applicability of regression they read further on the subject and visit one of the many elementary statistics texts available.

Simulations, Demonstrations, Interactions

Visit the Web site at: http://www.schoolsanddata.org and view dynamic demonstrations (movies) of both the SPSS and Excel procedures covered in this chapter. In addition, a PowerPoint presentation covering the important concepts of the chapter is available for your use.

APPLICATION ACTIVITY

Enter the following data into SPSS or Excel and conduct a regression analysis (be aware that two things should be done before one performs a regression analysis: (1) look at a scatterplot of the data, and (2) make certain that the correlation is significant).

Test Scores	GPA
98	2.1
105	2.4
100	3.2
100	2.7
106	2.2
95	2.3
116	2.8
112	3.4

NCLB ACTIVITY

One of the specific goals of No Child Left Behind (NCLB), as spelled out in the *Federal Register* issued on March 6, 2002, is, "By 2013–2014, all students will be proficient in reading by the end of third grade." Can you think of a way that regression analysis might help us to predict a student's reading proficiency? For example, suppose we find a very significant relationship (correlation) between the amount of time (minutes or hours) parents spent reading to students before kindergarten age and reading proficiency in Grade 3? In other words, the more time parents read to their child, the more likely the student will be proficient at reading in third grade.

Using something we call "backward mapping," interview or survey the parents of your third graders and seek answers to the question, "How often did you read stories to your child before entry to kindergarten?" Then conduct a correlation of those data and whether or not the child is proficient in reading. If there is a strong correlation, see if a regression analysis results in a fairly good model for predicting reading proficiency in third grade based on the time parents read to their child before kindergarten.

CHAPTER SIX

Formulating Research Questions and the Comparison of Means

I n the previous two chapters on correlation and regression, we specifically were interested in looking at how variables related to each other and, further, in predicting a particular outcome. We investigated the variables *as they were*. In other words, we observed variables in their present state.

Very often in education, we are interested in trying a new instructional strategy or method and then determining whether our new strategy has an effect on student learning. For example, we wonder if a new reading program that emphasizes "phonics" might be more effective than our current program in teaching third graders to become proficient in reading. In essence, we are changing or manipulating one variable (reading strategy) to see if it has a positive or negative effect on the other variable (reading proficiency).

Before we go further, it is critical that we distinguish between the *independent* and *dependent* variables. Let me try to help conceptualize a bit. The dependent variable is the one that measures or tests something—in this case, the measurement of reading proficiency. Obviously, this is usually some kind of test or assessment. On the other hand, the independent variable is the one we change, manipulate, or introduce—here, the introduction of the new phonics strategy. The research question becomes: Does the independent variable (phonics strategy) have an effect on the dependent variable (measurement of reading proficiency)? There are several ways to help us identify each, but I find it helpful to think in this way: the outcome on the test (dependent) is dependent on the particular type of teaching method (independent). Or as some of my students say, "We just memorize that the measurement is the dependent variable." I guess that is OK, but be aware that sometimes the identification of dependent and independent is based on how we set up or state our research questions. I think you will understand as we move through this chapter.

HYPOTHESIS TESTING AND FORMULATING RESEARCH QUESTIONS

In Chapter 4 of the first edition of *Schools and Data*, I spent considerable time discussing hypothesis testing. Over the years, the use of hypothesis testing has been replaced by the formulation of research questions. In both graduate classes and school settings, we find that dealing with research questions is more useful and easier to deal with than the more formal statements of null and alternative hypotheses. Even in the formal doctoral dissertation, we see more and more use of research questions rather than statements of null and alternative hypotheses. *So*, I focus more on the use of research questions throughout this chapter.

Before you allow some of this statistical terminology to scare you off, permit me to explain why educators might be interested in formulating research questions. First of all, stating the research question identifies the specific reason or purpose of the investigation. In addition, keeping focused on the question helps keep the study on track and avoids looking at variables or issues not related to the study. I suggest that we ask the kinds of questions every day that lend themselves to the formulation of research questions. A research question can help educators differentiate between real patterns in the data and patterns that may happen just by chance. For example, do students perform better in math if they have supplemental experiences with manipulatives, or do higher scores just result by chance? The purpose of the research question is to decide whether the results indicate a real relationship between two variables or whether the results are happening just by chance.

For example, our third grade teacher Karla in Chapter 1 had reason to suspect that her district's current math curriculum was not benefiting both her high- and low-achieving math students. She could not prove the suspicion, but she felt there was a pattern surfacing over the years with her third grade students. Let's help Karla create a couple of research questions:

Research Question 1. Will the students in Karla's third grade class who rank below average in math show a difference in math achievement over a 4-year period?

Research Question 2. Will the students in Karla's third grade class who rank above average in math show a difference in math achievement over a 4-year period?

You may think these two questions sound redundant or even rather simplistic. But staying focused on these two questions will get at the real heart of Karla's concern. And, she does not want to waste time collecting data that are not related to these questions. An analogy may be in order here.

I like to use the analogy of an hourglass (Figure 6.1) when I discuss the formulation of research questions.

Figure 6.1   Hourglass Analogy

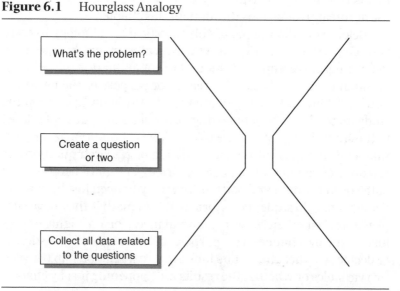

What's the problem?

Create a question or two

Collect all data related to the questions

It is critical that we as educators first identify the problem we want to investigate. This is not always an easy task, but is necessary before we can set our sights on the target. If the problem is not clear, specific, and well thought out, we run the risk of collecting and analyzing data unrelated to our problem, and in turn missing the real evidence that will help us answer the research question.

The top of the hourglass represents our thinking as we struggle with the importance and significance of our investigation. But we must then "narrow and refine" our thinking so it can be stated in a couple of very specific and focused questions. And then, in a sense, we branch out again, but this time to collect as much data as we can related to the specific formulated research questions.

Karla presented enough evidence (test scores) from her third grade classroom to indicate that the higher-level students in her class were achieving at a slower rate than the lower-level students in math.

In analyzing data around our research questions, there is danger of making an incorrect decision. Sometimes we conclude that the independent variable is having an effect on the dependent variable when in fact it is not. Using our phonics example, we run the risk of saying that the phonics strategy caused students to become more proficient in reading, when it was really some other variable that caused the effect. Conversely, sometimes we conclude that there was no effect caused by the independent variable, when in fact there was. We are talking about Type 1 and Type 2 errors here (more about these types of error in Chapter 7).

We will not get technical here, but you might ask, "OK, but how do we know if we made an error or not?" Hmmm . . . , we really do not know. In statistical analysis, there is always a chance that we will make the wrong decision. But then you ask, "So, why should we waste our time if there is so much chance of error?" Now the good news: as we will learn shortly, there are procedures we can use to reduce and we hope minimize the chance of making the wrong decision. To set the stage, we need to consider four basic steps to follow as we begin to formulate research questions and collect and analyze our data to help answer the questions:

1. State the research question or questions.

2. Decide on the criterion for a decision: How much of a difference is significant enough to draw a conclusion?

3. Collect your data and analyze.

4. Make a decision.

Z SCORES

Covering Step 1 was easy, as we found out in Karla's case study, but Step 2 requires familiarity with Z scores. Hang on, we will go slowly! It really is pretty simple. Reflecting back on our Morris Middle School math test scores in Chapter 3, recall that we had a set of data with a mean of 27 (27.16). The 135 individual test scores were considerably spread out, and individual student scores were not easily identified. Wouldn't it be nice if we could come up with a system of transforming all those 135 scores into a few simple numbers? Displayed in Figure 6.2 is a strategy for transforming all Morris Middle School test scores into something called "Z scores."

Figure 6.2   Normal Curve With 27 as a Z Score of 0

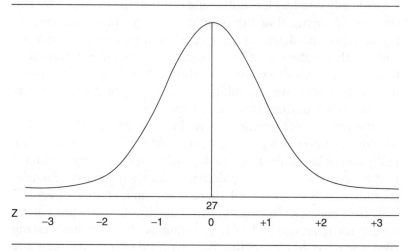

The mean of your set of scores (sample) is always transformed to zero. Keep in mind that this is just a way of transforming, so we can better understand our set of data, and more important, it gives us the ability to plot or identify each and every student's score in relationship to the mean. OK, so we call the mean zero—doesn't change the value, just a label of sorts. Values above the mean are

+1, +2, +3, and higher; values below the mean are −1, −2, −3, and lower. Because the numbers are continuous, Z scores can also fall between the numbers as decimals. As an example, a score of 28 (slightly higher than the mean of 27) will fall at approximately .30 as a Z score. Conversely, a score of 26 (slightly lower than the mean of 27) might be represented by a Z score of −.30.

A Note About the Distribution Curve

You will notice that in all of the figures displaying the normal curve, as the distance from the mean increases (in either a positive or negative direction), the ends or tails of the curve never actually touch the horizontal axis. This is because a theoretical distribution has an infinite range. Though Figure 6.2 (and others) might show a Z score range from −3 to +3, there are actually Z scores further out on the tail of the curve and beyond 3. Don't let a Z score of 3.9 fool you!

Why Are Z Scores Useful?

Suppose John, a Morris Middle School student, scored 32 on his math examination. How did he do? All that we can determine is that he scored *somewhere* above the mean of 27. But depending on the overall spread of the group, 32 may not be that impressive. We need more information—the mean itself is not enough to tell John the exact location of his score.

Remember our discussion of standard deviation in Chapter 3? And remember our brief mention of standard deviation as a number that represents a unit of measurement? A Z score of 1 is one of those units. So are 2 and 3 and all decimals (for example, 2.3) in between. *Oops!* So are −1, −2, and −3 (and decimals in between). Positive Z scores represent scores located above the mean, and negative Z scores represent scores located below the mean.

The standard deviation of our Morris Middle School math scores is 5 (5.01). This number represents one standard deviation unit (+1 above the mean and −1 below the mean). So the mean (27) plus 5 points (32) falls on a Z score of +1 (above the mean). The mean (27) minus 5 points (22) falls on a Z score of −1 (below the mean). John's score of 32 has a Z score of +1. This helps us pinpoint the exact location of his specific score. The formula follows, and a more visual presentation is shown in Figure 6.3.

$$Z = \frac{student\ score - mean}{deviation} = \frac{32 - 27}{5} = \frac{5}{5} = 1$$

Figure 6.3   Standard Deviation and Z Score

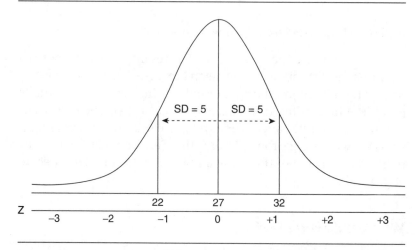

The numerator in the equation measures the distance between the score and the mean and indicates whether the score is above (+) or below (–) the mean. We divide this distance by the standard deviation because we want the Z score to measure distance in terms of standard deviation units. Recall that the purpose of the Z score is to specify the exact location in the distribution. This formula calculates the direction (+ or –) and the distance from the mean.

We also know that all of the scores falling between one standard deviation unit below the mean (25) and one standard deviation unit above the mean (32) represent approximately 68% of the entire sample of scores. If this is not clear, hang in there—we talk more about Z scores in a moment.

Relating Hypothesis Testing to Research Questions

When we do hypothesis testing (or investigate our research questions), we use data from a sample to test our hypothesis. Our data gives us evidence or reason either to accept or reject our hypothesis. If there is a *significant discrepancy* between our data and the claim of no difference (null hypothesis), we have support for accepting our research or alternative hypothesis and can claim that there is really a difference. Think for a moment about Karla's case study. She found a significant discrepancy between the district's claim of no difference and her data collection and analysis. And based on the criterion she set (Step 2), she made the decision to reject the null hypothesis of no difference and accepted her research hypothesis of significant difference.

But how do we decide what constitutes a reason to accept or reject? Our job in Step 2 is to create a logical criterion for making this decision. Our data (sample) must be so different and represent such a significant discrepancy from the normal population that we are justified in making a decision in favor of our research hypothesis or research questions. If we cannot show a significant difference, then we are not justified in accepting our research hypothesis and therefore must conclude that our independent variable did not have a significant effect on our dependent variable. In Karla's case, if she did not find significant difference between how the lower- and higher-level students progressed in math, she would be justified in accepting the district's position that the math curriculum was effective for both levels of students.

Z scores, in combination with what are called *probability values* or *alpha levels,* will enable us to determine what constitutes a significant difference. Let's take time out and look at an example.

As superintendent of the Westside School District, I have a suspicion that our graduating seniors have a significantly higher grade point average (GPA) than the average senior in Fresno County, California. It is true, the difference in GPA between our seniors and the county's average must be significantly different for me to be justified in calling the *Fresno Bee* to publicize our success. The real question is, How different do the GPAs have to be? This gets us to Step 2—setting the criterion for making a decision. First, let me complete Step 1 and state the research question:

Is there a significant difference between Westside seniors' GPA and the Fresno County average?

To be justified in providing an answer (or accepting the research hypothesis) to this research question, I must show considerable evidence and significant difference in the GPAs. If our seniors' GPA average (mean) is only a few points higher, the critics will say that it could have happened by chance. Just a coincidence, they will say!

I must determine what constitutes a low probability of chance as opposed to a high probability of chance. You'll remember that this specific probability value (*p*) is a statistical term called *level of significance* or the *alpha level*. In education, we use two common probability values: .05 and .01. Simply, .05 means that there is less than a 5% chance that the result could have happened by chance alone. And with an alpha level of .01, there is less than a 1% chance that our result happened by chance alone. Obviously, the .01 alpha level will be more stringent and difficult to meet. But, if so, it increases the *power* and *significance* of our finding. Yeah, I know, sounds complicated, huh?

You can see that if we set our criterion at .01 we can be more certain that our research question (or research hypothesis) is true and we will risk less chance of error in our decision. However, it can also be argued that meeting the .01 alpha level is much more difficult, and may result in missing *practical significance*.

Practical Significance? What Is That?

Just as an example of practical significance, let's suppose your child's teacher implements a new reading strategy to improve reading comprehension. As a result of her study, she determines that there is not enough evidence to conclude that the majority of students benefit from the new strategy. But, what if *your child* happened to benefit from the new method? Maybe not for the majority of the class, but the strategy resulted in a significant effect on your child. So, what happens if we make a decision to discard the new strategy? *Oops*—to the detriment of your child. You see, maybe there was not enough evidence for statistical significance, but *practically* there was an effect on one child.

Take another example: A new drug is being tested to determine the cure for Parkinson's disease. A sample of 100 elderly patients participate in the study. At the conclusion of the study, there is insufficient evidence that the new drug showed any effect on the majority of the sample. *But,* what if 2 of the 100 patients had a positive reaction to the drug and eventually returned to a more normal condition. Get it? Statistically speaking, maybe the evidence was not strong enough to show significance—*but*, in reality, two human beings were positively affected by the independent variable (drug). Would we not argue that for these two individuals (especially if they were our parents or grandparents) there was a significant effect caused by the independent variable? Statistically significant, maybe not—but *practically*, you better believe it! More on practical significance later. Yep, and we will talk briefly about something called *effect sizes* and *confidence levels*.

These extremely unlikely levels (.01 and .05), along with a Z score, will help us identify what are called *critical regions*. If our findings fall within these critical regions, they will be inconsistent with the null hypothesis (no significant difference) and will lend support for our research question: Is there a difference in GPAs? Whenever our sample data produce a mean score that is so different from the population mean that it falls in the *critical region* of the distribution, we can reject the null hypothesis of no difference and accept our research hypothesis (or question).

Figure 6.4 shows how Z scores and alpha levels are used together to determine the critical region. If your sample mean falls at or beyond the Z score of −1.96 or +1.96 at a probability level of .05,

Figure 6.4　Critical Region at .05 Alpha Level

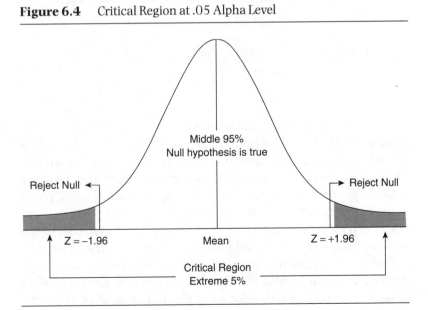

your sample falls in the critical region and allows you to accept your research hypothesis or question. The sample is different enough and shows a significant discrepancy between the normal population and your sample that can justify the decision to reject the notion of no difference and accept your research hypothesis or question.

If, on the other hand, the sample mean corresponds to a Z score of less than the 1.96, the difference is not enough to be significant and does not warrant a decision to reject the hypothesis of "no difference"—on the contrary, in this case, the no difference position must be retained. In addition, our result suggests more than a 5% chance that the result could have happened by chance alone. *Oops!* Not something I feel confident about.

Let's go back to my hypothesis or research question that asks if the Westside School seniors have significantly higher GPAs than the Fresno County average (mean). Suppose the population (Fresno County) mean GPA is 2.5 with a standard deviation of 0.5. Westside seniors have a mean GPA of 3.2. We first of all know that the sample mean is higher than the population mean, but the real question is, Does the difference show a significant discrepancy, and is the difference great enough that we can say the result is significant at the .05 alpha level? Figure 6.5 shows our sample mean of 3.2 transformed to a Z score of 1.4 along with the critical regions for a .05 alpha level. I include here the formula and calculation of the Z score.

$$Z = \frac{sample\ mean - population\ mean}{deviation} = \frac{3.2 - 2.5}{.5} = \frac{.7}{.5} = 1.4$$

Our sample mean of 3.2 (Z score of 1.4) does not fall in the extreme part of the distribution tail identified by 1.96, so it is not different enough for me to accept my alternative hypothesis. Though Westside seniors' GPAs are higher than the county's mean, the difference is not significant. In essence, the difference could have resulted by chance or error. Doing some quick math in your head probably tells you that our seniors would need a mean of 3.5 (Z score of 2.0) to fall into the critical region and thus be different enough to reject no difference and accept a significant difference. You may also see that if the standard deviation were smaller (less spread out)—for example, 0.3 instead of 0.5—the

Figure 6.5   Critical Region for Z = 1.4

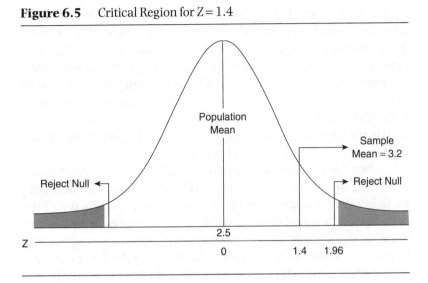

resulting Z score would be 2.3, high enough to fall into the critical region at or beyond 1.9. (Excuse me while I contact my secretary and have her cancel that call to the *Fresno Bee* making my somewhat premature announcement.)

THE *t* STATISTIC

Before introducing the *t* statistic, let's recap a bit regarding our procedure for using the Z score method. The procedure involved (1) the assumption that the sample mean and the population mean would be similar, (2) the use of standard error to determine how much difference between the two means could be expected just by chance, and (3) the calculation of a Z score to determine if the obtained result would be significantly greater than would be expected by chance. In our Westside GPA example, if the resulting Z score fell within the middle 95% of the distribution, it was not significant enough to occur by chance alone. On the other hand, if the resulting Z score fell at or into the critical region (+ or −1.96), the sample was significantly different and was not likely (.05) to have occurred by chance. Recall that the alpha level of .05 means that the result could have occurred by chance 5 or fewer times out of 100.

So we wonder: If the Z score method works in this example, why do we need this thing called a t statistic? The answer is really quite simple. To calculate a Z score, we must know the standard deviation (or variance) of the population. In our previous example, the population standard deviation for the county was 0.5. But in most cases we do not know the standard deviation of the population. Without the standard deviation, we cannot compute the standard error and cannot calculate the amount of expected difference between the sample mean and the population mean.

When the population standard deviation is absent, the t statistic is used instead of the Z score. In actuality, the t statistic allows us to *estimate* the standard error of the population by using the sample standard deviation—providing an estimate of the distance between the sample mean and the population mean. Again, it is beyond the scope of this chapter to list the formulas for calculating the t statistic. With the help of a t statistical table (Resource B) and SPSS or Excel, the calculation of the t statistic is quite simple.

Before we work with a real-life situation, we need to touch lightly on the concept of *degrees of freedom*. Degrees of freedom (*df*) is a number that describes the numbers of values (scores) that are free to vary in that distribution (sample). To simplify, suppose you have a distribution of three scores and you know that the sum is 30. If you assign two of the three values—10 and 15—the third value is not free to vary because it must be 5 to achieve the sum of 30. Given the two values, $10 + 15 = 25$, and the sum is 30, the third value must equal 5. The point is that the third value is not free to vary. Just remember, the *df* for a distribution of a sample variable is equal to the sample number minus 1. In our Westside GPA example, $df = 19$ $(20 - 1)$. The practical implication for using degrees of freedom is that using $N - 1$ results in a smaller t value, reducing the risk of underestimating the standard error. Important to realize is that the sample size itself *is not* reduced—we only subtract a number from N before the t statistic is calculated. All 20 scores remain in the sample. Kind of like instead of dividing by 20, let's divide by 19—to better estimate the standard error. This is particularly the case with small sample sizes. As you can see, the greater the value of *df* for a distribution, the closer the sample variance represents the population variance, and the better the t statistic approximates the Z score. No surprise here—the larger the sample, the more accurate we can answer our research questions or reject or accept the hypothesis.

ONE-SAMPLE *t* TEST: AN EXAMPLE

We return to our Westside seniors and will use a *t* statistic rather than a Z score to test the research hypothesis that our GPA mean score is significantly different from the Fresno County average. To simplify the procedure, let's use a small sample of 20 seniors. Table 6.1 displays their GPA scores. This might be a good place to start with creating your own file and work along with me. In both SPSS and Excel, simply input the GPAs in a column—there is no need to input the 20 students, since you can use the numbered left-hand side of the file for this purpose.

Table 6.1   Westside GPA Scores

Student	GPA	Student	GPA
1	2.5	11	3.3
2	2.8	12	2.9
3	2.6	13	2.4
4	2.9	14	2.3
5	2.4	15	2.5
6	2.5	16	2.7
7	2.7	17	2.5
8	2.9	18	2.8
9	3.1	19	2.9
10	3.2	20	3.0

Let's follow the four steps mentioned earlier.

1. State the null and research hypotheses (or your research questions).

   Null: The mean GPA of Westside seniors is not significantly different from the county average of 2.5.

   Research: The mean GPA of Westside seniors is significantly different from the county average of 2.5.

2. Determine the degrees of freedom (*df*) and locate the critical region as criteria *for making a decision.* We identify the critical region of the distribution where the *t* value of our sample mean must fall to be considered significant. Selecting an alpha level of .05, we look at Resource B to determine the critical *t* value associated with 19 degrees of freedom (sample minus 1). This value is 2.09 for an alpha level of .05. We will compare the observed sample *t* value to the critical value of 2.09.

3. Analyze the data. In this step, we (SPSS or Excel, actually) calculate the observed *t* value of our Westside seniors—please trust that it was calculated correctly and the result is 3.89.

4. Make a decision. From Step 2, we recall that for our sample data to be statistically significant, the obtained *t* value must be 2.09 or greater. In this case, the observed *t* value of 3.89 is greater than the critical value (2.09), so we can (with somewhat confidence) reject the null and accept our research hypothesis—that our seniors' GPA is significantly higher than the country average. *Note:* You may ask why I stated "with somewhat confidence" when the test clearly revealed a significance. In the next chapter, I discuss two new concepts: (1) power and (2) effect size. These two concepts help identify a more specific *degree of confidence* or power of our finding. OK, let's see how SPSS or Excel can help us.

This particular *t* test is called a "one-sample *t* test." Recall that we said that a *t* test requires two samples. Technically, we do have two here (the Westside seniors and the county average). Don't let this confuse you, because we are really comparing one sample (seniors) and a second one (the Fresno County average). For this one example, I want to focus on the use of SPSS, since this software allows us to input the data in a one-sample way, comparing the mean to another mean called a "test value." Excel does not have this special feature, but will be available to us as we move into the next chapter, the independent-samples *t* test.

SPSS

First, you must create a file in SPSS using the data from Figure 6.6. Simply insert the GPA scores in the first column—no need to put the individual student identification in the file, since we can use the existing number on the left menu of the file. Select **Analyze** on the menu bar, then select **Compare Means.** Choose a **One-Sample *t*-Test,** highlight the variable GPA, and move to the right side of the screen. You will notice that the Test Value Box defaults to 0. Type **2.5** (population mean) in this box, and select **OK**. (You can visit the *Schools and Data* Web site at: http://www.schoolsanddata .org and view the simulation for this procedure.)

Figure 6.6   SPSS One-Sample Test

				Test Value = 2.5		
					95% Confidence Interval of the Difference	
	t	df	Sig. (2-tailed)	Mean Difference	Lower	Upper
GPA	3.88	19	.001	.2450	.1240	.3860

You will first notice that SPSS prints out some descriptive statistics such as sample number, mean, and standard deviation. The box below the descriptive information displays the significance (or lack of) of the *t* test. Mean difference is the difference between the observed sample mean (2.745) and the population mean (2.5). The important question: Is a mean difference of .2450 large enough to be considered significantly different from 2.5? The results of the *t* test reveal that *t* = 3.88, with 19 (*N*−1) degrees of freedom (*df*). The significance (.001) represents an alpha level much less than our chosen .05. We can reject the null and accept our research hypothesis for a couple of reasons: (1) the *t* value of 3.88 is well into the critical region of 2.09 (selected from the *t* statistical table in Resource B), and (2) the test is significant at an even lower alpha level (.001) than the one we chose (.05).

CONCLUSION

Both the Z-score and the *t*-statistic tests are used to test hypotheses between sample and population data, and to answer research questions. The reason for using the t test in most instances relates to the information that we do not usually have—the population variance. The t test allows us to analyze data when we have little information about the population. The real advantage of the t test is that we can test our research hypothesis or answer research questions with just a null hypothesis and a sample from a perhaps little-known population.

With the enormous amount of school data we collect (and most often have stored on a shelf someplace), such as standardized test scores, average daily attendance (ADA), grades, and dropout figures, the t statistic lends itself very nicely to improving the decision-making process through the use of school data. In Chapter 7, we will learn how to use this same t statistic with more than one sample—the independent-samples t test. Again, both SPSS and Excel will simplify the procedure and continue to make our lives easier. Analyzing data is one thing—but being able to do so and still have time in our professional lives to concentrate on data interpretation and implications for school improvement is quite another.

APPLICATION ACTIVITY

As a sixth grade teacher, you are concerned about the pre-algebra test that your class has to take at the end of the year in preparation for seventh grade. Their performance determines placement in pre-algebra or general math. The district scores for students placed in pre-algebra over the past several years reveal a mean score of 92 and a standard deviation of 4. After several weeks of preparation, you administer a practice test to your sixth graders. The result is a mean score of 94. Is the mean difference significant enough to lead you to believe that your class is ready to pass the pre-algebra test in May?

NCLB ACTIVITY

One of the No Child Left Behind (NCLB) requirements is that you shall conduct annual testing of all students against state standards in math and reading in Grades 3–8. Let's suppose you want to compare your district's third graders' scores in reading with the state's average. How could a one-sample t test help you with your investigation? Obviously, you would want to find out what the state's average is—not difficult to get either from your state education Web site or with a simple phone call.

CHAPTER SEVEN

The Independent-Samples t Test

M uch of what we want to know in education involves two samples rather than just one. For instance, we often want to compare two methods of instruction, such as phonics instruction versus the whole language approach. Do students learn science better or faster if they are exposed to instruction in the field as opposed to others who receive instruction only in the traditional classroom setting? Do limited-English-speaking students who receive English as a second language (ESL) instruction become more proficient at speaking English than limited-English-speaking students who do not receive ESL instruction? As you can guess, most research studies involve comparison of two (or more) samples or data sets. Sometimes our sample is the same, but we are exposing the same students to two different methods of instruction, which in fact gives us two separate data sets. These kinds of studies are called "independent measures research designs," meaning that they analyze the mean difference between the two samples. The statistical test used in this kind of study is also called the "independent measures t statistic." More on this later.

A TRY AT CONCEPTUAL UNDERSTANDING

The driving force and real purpose of *Schools and Data* are to provide you with as much conceptual knowledge of statistical analysis as

I can. So I want to take some time here to paint a conceptual picture of the *t* test and the rationale for using it in our schools as we pursue school improvement and increased student learning.

I have stated elsewhere that traditional approaches to statistical analysis have failed the general population (including myself) for many reasons. I will not discuss these many reasons in detail here—we all have a pretty good idea what some of them are—but let me state briefly that we were taught in a theoretical atmosphere of hard-to-understand formulas and with too few examples of applicability to the work we do in schools. My personal interest in the use of data in schools surfaced only after I began to ask conceptual questions of *when, where, and why would I use this stuff?* Forget the complex formulas for a minute—I first need a conceptualization (a picture if you will) of the procedure and its applicability.

Most of what we investigate in schools relates to differences. You know! What is the difference between whole language and phonics instruction? Can I design a new discipline plan for my elementary school that reduces office referrals and increases appropriate behavior in the classrooms? But, when we draw a conclusion that our new discipline program is effective, the real question must be, "Compared to what?" In other words, if we say our new discipline plan has resulted in 20% fewer office referrals—we must ask, "Compared to what?" Well, compared to data collected under our former discipline plan, or compared to data collected when we had no plan at all. The point is that we must have two groups of subjects (or two dependent variables measured on the same group)— and the *t* test compares the means of these two groups.

Let's stay with our new discipline plan for a minute. Just knowing that the result is 20% fewer office referrals may not be significantly different than the old plan—and maybe the difference is due to teachers suddenly handling their own discipline problems in their rooms. I am getting at a couple of things here: (1) the requirements for using the *t* test, and (2) the caution not to assume cause and effect. Significant difference is one thing; cause and effect is quite another. Looking briefly at some of the requirements for using the *t* test will help us with the *when, where,* and *why* questions.

Before we get to the procedure, let's talk about four kinds of data scales: (1) nominal, (2) ordinal, (3) interval, and (4) ratio. The distinctions among the four kinds of data are important because certain statistical procedures are used with some and not others. For example, a requirement of the *t* test is that the data are at least on the *interval* scale. Let me explain.

A *nominal scale* (meaning "having to do with names") consists of categories that have different names. For example, collecting data on gender results in categories of *male* and *female*. There is no quantitative or numerical quality to these categories—they are just names for individuals. Further, as we code these data, we assign another *name* to them as we input the data into SPSS or Excel (for example, male = 1; female = 2).

An *ordinal scale* (meaning "having to do with ranks") consists of categories that are organized in an ordered sequence. For example, on a survey, we ask students to rank their favorite menu items (for example, pizza, hot dogs, salad bar). So the student responds: first, second, and third. Though these data have a number quality to them (order), they do not reveal any magnitude of the difference between the numbers.

An *interval scale* consists of categories that have a series of *intervals* between them that are of equal size. In other words, there are actual numbers (or decimals) between each of the recorded data. Our often-used test scores fall into this data scale. The advantage of interval data allows us to compute distances between values and compute averages or means. Sometimes an interval scale goes below zero, as in above and below sea level. There is no absolute zero.

A *ratio scale* differs from the interval scale only in that it is a scale with an *absolute zero point.* In other words, the value of zero indicates none (a complete absence) of the variable being measured. A good example of a ratio scale is the measurement of students' height. There is a point that represents no height or the absence of the variable being measured (absolute zero). For example, I am 5 feet 6 inches in height. Further, my waist to my ankles measures 36 inches. Get it? The measurement scale consists of lots of numbers (inches and even half- and quarter-inches). The intervals throughout the scale are *even.* But, there exists a zero representing no height at all.

Requirements for the *t* Test

1. You must have two separate sets of data (for example, math scores for class A and math scores for class B). We call this procedure the "independent-samples *t* test," but recall our

use in Chapter 6 of the one-sample *t* test. Though we only had one sample, we actually had two means—a sample mean (Westside seniors' GPA) and a population mean (Fresno County average).

2. The sample means must be randomly selected. "Stacking the deck" with just the students from the gifted and talented class, or picking all the girls for one of the groups would not be appropriate and would likely result in incorrect conclusions. We must always control for as much as we can against our enemies—Type 1 and Type 2 error (discussed more later in the chapter).

3. The standard deviations of the two samples must be somewhat similar. This is another way of saying that the two sample distributions should be shaped similarly. Recall that the standard deviation is a measure of spread—if Sample 1 has a standard deviation of 10, and Sample 2 has a standard deviation of 30, the second sample is a much flatter (spread-out) distribution. Conducting *t* tests with two such dissimilar samples would again likely result in error and cause us to draw incorrect conclusions (and further cause us to make incorrect decisions about student learning).

4. Comparison between the two groups must be made on the same measure. We would not use a *t* test to compare a group's math scores with the other group's science scores. Recall that we did investigate two variables in this way with relationships (correlation).

5. The data used in *t* tests must be *interval* or *ratio* data—remember the four kinds: (1) nominal, (2) ordinal, (3) interval, and (4) ratio. Later, we will cover a common procedure used with nominal data—the chi-square statistic.

Power

In addition to calculating a *t* value, and deciding whether or not it is significant, we want to consider the *power* of such a finding. We have been discussing the importance of determining whether differences between groups are really different enough to be considered as *significantly* different. And recall Step 2 of our procedure: Decide on a criteria to make a decision. Up to this point, we have utilized an alpha level (.05) with all of our tests, which means the probability of being right if making a decision in favor of our new reading program, the teaching strategies used in a classroom, or the new discipline plan implemented at our school. Allow me to be a bit more technical and state it this way: The alpha level is the probability of being wrong when we reject the null hypothesis (of no difference). In other words, we are accepting a 5% chance of making an incorrect decision about rejecting the notion of no differences between our two groups (which is the same as saying that we decide that our new program is having a positive effect on student achievement).

Now remember—whenever we make a statistical decision (accept or reject a program) there is always a probability of being wrong. This is because *all* statistical decisions are based on the probability model. Hang on, a little more technical stuff here.

There are basically two kinds or categories of possible error: Type 1 and Type 2. If we *falsely reject* the null hypothesis of no difference, when in fact it is true, we have committed Type 1 error. If, on the other hand, we *falsely accept* the null hypothesis of no difference, when in fact there is significant difference between or among our groups, we have committed Type 2 error. The frustration here is that we really never are sure if we have committed error. But fortunately, there are ways to reduce the risk or chance of making both of these kinds of error. We already know how to reduce the risk of Type 1 error—that's set by the alpha level (for example, .05).

Now, since we know that alpha sets the level of Type 1 error, we need to think of how we can reduce the risk of Type 2 error. *Aha!* Statisticians to the rescue again. Turns out that the stats folks tell us there is something called *beta,* and this number addresses the risk of making Type 2 error. We'll see an example of how this is used in the next chapter when we conduct analysis of variance (ANOVA) among several groups.

For now, consider three things that can negatively affect the power of your finding:

1. *Skewness.* You know, if the majority of your students score high on their exam, they are piled up toward the high side of your distribution. Or maybe the opposite—the majority of your students failed the exam, and are piled up toward

the low side of the distribution. If your samples are skewed in either direction, you can be less confident in making a correct decision based on the t test results (for example, high t value with $p < .05$).

2. *Unequal variances within your sample.* Let's suppose you did not randomly select the students in your groups and you are comparing a group of gifted students with a group of low achievers. Get it! The variances within the gifted class would be drastically different than the variances within your low-achieving class. So, to increase the *power* of your test, try for as much equal variance within your sample groups. Randomization is the best way to control for this danger.

3. *Outliers.* An *outlier* is an individual score that is drastically different than the others. For example, let's say you were measuring SAT scores as the dependent variable (test score). Let's further suppose that in your sample was a student with a perfect score of 1600. Can you imagine how that one extreme score would affect the mean of the entire group? In a sense, it will skew the average toward the higher end and perhaps cause you to make an error in decision based on the mean of the group. So, what to do? It is appropriate under such conditions to eliminate that one score from your sample before you test for significance.

Effect Size (Independent-Samples *t* Test)

We cannot dismiss power without mentioning the importance of something called *effect size*. First of all, let me confess to you that many of us who study or teach statistics and research methods find it difficult to fully understand conceptually what effect size really is. So, if this is the case with you, do not worry or stress out. My intent is to make you aware of its importance and suggest that you consult other texts (my favorite is *Basic Statistical Analysis* by Richard Sprinthall [2000] to get a good grasp on the concept. However, let me try my best in explaining it to you.

Starting with an example may help. Let's suppose that we find an afterschool tutorial program results in the increase of high school students' GPA from 2.5 to 2.6. And we know from the state Web site that the population of high school students has a standard deviation of 2. The question is, What is the size (or power) of your treatment effect (that is, how powerful is the effect of your afterschool program to change GPA from 2.5 to 2.6)?

Formally defined, *effect size* is the difference between two means in units of population standard deviation. So, in our example here, the effect size of our afterschool tutorial program is 2.6 −2.5 / 2; where 2.6 is the sample result, 2.5 is the population mean, and 2 is the population standard deviation. The result of our equation is .50, or an effect size of .50. Now, what does this mean?

Well, the literature of research (and statistics texts) tells us that when using a *t* test, an effect size is considered small at .20; medium at .50; and strong at .80 or greater (Sprinthall, 2000). So, we have a medium effect size in our study, which means that we can be reasonably confident in rejecting the null of no significance when in fact that is truly the case (reducing the chance of Type 2 error).

Remember, the larger the effect size, the higher is the likelihood of detecting significant differences through the use of statistical procedures. And failing to consider effect size increases the risk of making incorrect decisions with our data analysis and interpretation. If we find significant differences in our studies, it is important to examine such differences to determine if our findings are meaningful or even useful.

The good news is that we do not have to mathematically calculate the effect size for a *t* test—SPSS will do it for us. But we do need to know the level of importance: effect size of .20 is considered small; .50 is considered medium; and .80 is considered great. And be aware that the level of importance is slightly different for each kind of statistical test. This discussion has focused on the effect size levels for the *t* test. Estimating the effect size for correlation is pretty straightforward—it is r^2. Remember back in Chapter 4 we said that r^2 is a number that describes the amount of *effect* that one variable has on another variable. Yep! You're right—that is effect size. And in the next chapter we discover an easy way (using SPSS) to estimate the effect size with ANOVA.

Oops! One More Thing

What I am now going to say may seem to you as complicating the issue. But, I contend that in actuality it will simplify things. Sometimes we overemphasize the theoretical and neglect the practical. The same holds true with our interpretation of statistical test results. For example, we may have studied the use of phonics instruction in Grades 1–3 over time and found that the difference was somewhat small and even appeared to be trivial (slightly significant). OK, but what if the instructional strategy helped a few students read and write better? And what if you were the parent of one of these few? Get it? The effect would certainly be significant to you, right? So again, we say that the real essence of statistics is one's interpretation of the findings. And in addition, since there is always the risk of error, we must be careful about the conclusions we draw from our studies. So you may say, "Then why do we even bother with statistical testing when there is so much risk of error, absence of power, low effect sizes, and misinterpretations of the findings?"

Let me respond by asking you to think about the testing of the relationship between smoking and lung cancer—not recent testing, but testing that occurred 50 years ago. At the beginning stages of testing, results revealed a very small relationship, with a very small effect size, and even implied that there was *no relationship*. And each study seemed to contradict the one before. The point is that only with repeated testing over time, increased sample sizes, and reducing the number of confounding variables did we arrive at *now* an extremely strong correlation, with extremely high effect sizes, and a very confident conclusion of the effect of smoking on lung cancer.

Now, jump to our field (education) for a moment. We have a pretty good idea (maybe a low to medium effect size) about how students become effective readers and writers and productive citizens in our society. But, we do not necessarily have real strong evidence (strong effect size) of what strategies work and what strategies do not work. So, I say that we may be in a similar place in time as the medical profession 50 years ago. We are passionate, dedicated educators and we care deeply about educating children to their fullest potential. *Why should we bother?* We all know the answer. We'll study and investigate what works—and continue to look for the variables and strategies that increase student learning and school improvement. And, we are not likely to find *all* of the answers, but perhaps we'll find *some* of them!

Remember how we talked in Chapter 6 about the difference between the mean of a sample and the mean of a population? We also, especially with the Z score method, compared the standard error of a sample and population. The results of our testing looked very closely at the differences between the means and standard errors of the sample and population.

If we are now going to look at two independent samples, can you see that we probably will be interested in looking at these same components between the two independent samples? So we are really looking at something like the following:

The mean of one sample compared to the mean of another sample compared to the population mean—then all of this related to the standard error of one sample compared to the standard error of the other sample.

Again, we will not get into the formula in detail, but actually the formula was just stated in words. I hope that you will gain a general conceptual idea of what happens in an independent-samples *t* test. The following example may help.

A Personal Hypothesis or Research Question

Allow me to share a personal story and how perhaps we can use the independent-sample *t* statistic to test my hypothesis or answer my research question. Several years ago, I taught a course called "Applied Quantitative Methods" (a fancy term for applied educational statistics) to teacher education majors at a university. My instruction was delivered in a very traditional classroom setting, focusing primarily on the textbook, and involved a lot of lecture from the instructor. Most of the examples used in class were not from the field of education but from psychology and other social sciences (I was only following the textbook . . .). I still have in my files the students' final examinations.

A few years later, I accepted a position at another major university, and I currently teach a similar course to aspiring and practicing teachers and principals. But my instructional delivery has changed dramatically. I lecture less, and I have students complete in-the-field assignments involving their own data sets. The examples I use in class are specific to education, and I request that students bring their data sets from their schools. Though we use the textbook, it serves as more of a guide as we *roll up our sleeves* and mess with data from our workplace.

Research Question: Are the student exam scores from University A significantly higher (on average) than the exam scores from University B?

Let's walk through our familiar four steps before we proceed:

Step 1. State the Research
Question in the Form of a Hypothesis

I am beginning to sense that my present students are attaining higher grades on their final examination. Perhaps this is because of my increased years of experience with teaching this course, but I want to test the hypothesis that my students at University A are achieving at a higher level than my former students at University B. If so, I want to further investigate whether or not this may be due to my different instructional delivery method. Let's specifically state the research hypothesis designed from my earlier research question.

Research Hypothesis: The sample means from my two groups of students (University A and University B) are not equal and therefore will be statistically significantly different.

I have taken a random sample of 20 students from each of the two universities. Their final exam scores appear in Table 7.1.

Time to test your skills again—create your own file with these data in either Excel or SPSS. I have titled mine "University *t* Test." (See Figure 7.1.) In both Excel and SPSS, enter the numbers 1–40 in Column 1 or use the left menu bar as student numbers (1–40). In Column 2, enter a coding number for each of the universities (that is, a 1 for University B and a 2 for University A). Remember, our software doesn't deal with or understand words very well—we need a number representing each word. Now, in the third column, record each exam score for each of the 40 students. Here's a view of the data set in SPSS. As you see, I chose to use the left menu bar in place of the 1–40 students, placed my coding in Column 1, and placed the respective exam scores in Column 2.

Step 2. Decide the Criteria for Making a Decision

Before I check the *t* statistic table in Resource B to identify the critical region and alpha level, let me point out to you that there will be two separate degrees of freedom (*df*). Can you guess why? Correct—because there are two independent samples, we will have $(n - 1)$ plus $(n - 1)$. There is one score in each sample that is not free to vary. It is important to realize that when we use degrees of

Table 7.1   Final Exam Scores for University A and University B
Sample Students

Student	University	Score	Student	University	Score
1	A	85	21	B	80
2	A	93	22	B	70
3	A	87	23	B	93
4	A	72	24	B	58
5	A	71	25	B	85
6	A	90	26	B	85
7	A	61	27	B	87
8	A	88	28	B	84
9	A	92	29	B	74
10	A	82	30	B	72
11	A	89	31	B	83
12	A	88	32	B	72
13	A	73	33	B	88
14	A	91	34	B	89
15	A	85	35	B	86
16	A	83	36	B	61
17	A	88	37	B	68
18	A	87	38	B	70
19	A	85	39	B	82
20	A	83	40	B	58

Figure 7.1   University t Test

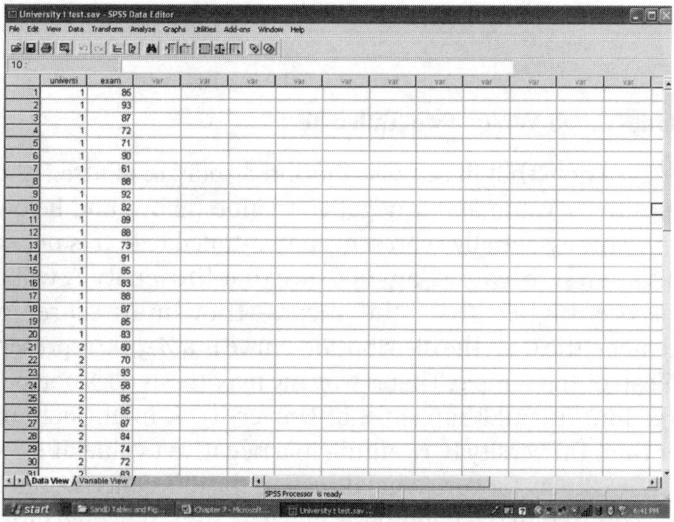

freedom, we are not discarding the two scores—the purpose is to reduce the number by one before calculating the *t* value. In a sense, by reducing the number before calculation of the formula, we are reducing the risk of error. More on this later. So, with degrees of freedom 38, and an alpha level of .05, we see in Resource B a critical region of approximately 2.03 (between 30 and 40). This means that our resulting *t* value from our test needs to be 2.03 or greater (out in the tail of the distribution) to be considered statistically significant. In other words, in order for me to accept my hypothesis of a significant difference between my two samples, the resulting *t* value must be 2.03 or greater. Figure 7.2 helps clarify.

Figure 7.2   Curve and Critical Region

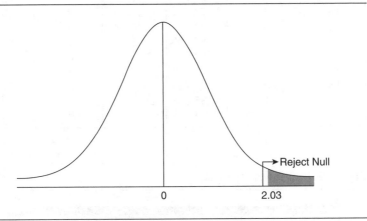

One-Tailed Versus Two-Tailed Test

One-Tailed Versus Two-Tailed Test

Please note that in our distribution display in Figure 7.2 there is a positive *t* value and a negative *t* value (above and below the mean). This essentially represents a two-tailed test. It is necessary in this analysis because I am not sure that University A will actually score higher than the mean—they may score lower. Remember, the 0 on the distribution curve is a Z *score* representing the mean of the sample. That is why my hypothesis does not indicate a direction. It could happen that University A might actually be lower than University B, resulting in a negative *t* value. If for some reason, we knew for sure what direction the difference would likely be, we could state the hypothesis in a way that indicated direction (positive or negative). Not surprisingly, this would be called a *directional hypothesis* and utilize a one-tailed test. Now that I have covered this, I strongly recommend using a two-tailed test always— *yikes!* But you need to be aware of the difference (as you will see the option in SPSS and Excel).

Step 3. Analyze the Data

Again, you must trust that I correctly calculated (with formula) the observed t value to be 2.123. A bit later, we will bring SPSS and Excel to the rescue.

Step 4. Make a Decision

The observed t value for the comparison of my two samples is 2.123, just a tad higher than the critical value of 2.03 (Wow! Pretty close). And with a significance of .04, it meets the selected .05 criteria. Technically, I can accept my research hypothesis at the .05 level of significance.

Using SPSS and Excel for Testing Independent Samples

SPSS

You should have already created an SPSS file from the data in Table 7.1. From the menu bar, select **Analyze**, then choose **Compare Means.** This time, select **Independent Samples t-Test.**

You will need to move the dependent variable final exam (scores column) to the Test Variable box on the right side of the screen (single-click on the exam and move into the box with the highlighted arrow). You will then move the independent variable (university column) to the **Grouping Variable** box. Get it? You need to tell SPSS what the codes for your two groups are (that is, University A = 1; University B = 2). The term *grouping variable* should help with the definition because you will "group" the university variable. After you move the University variable to the Grouping Variable box, you will notice the **Define Group** button highlighted. Here is where you tell SPSS how you want your groups defined. Simply select **Define Groups** and type in "1" for Group 1 and "2" for Group 2. Click on **Continue,** then **OK,** to return to the original t test screen.

Clicking **OK** on the original screen results in your independent-samples *t* test analysis, shown in Figure 7.3. (Don't forget, there is a simulation of this procedure on the *Schools and Data* Web site at: http://www.schoolsanddata .org.)

SPSS first gives you some descriptive data (for example, number in samples, means, standard deviation, and standard error) on the dependent variable (exam score) for each of the two university samples (A and B), shown in the box called "Group Statistics" in Figure 7.3. (We will not deal with the Levene's test for equality in this book.) A bit to the right (in the box called "Independent-Samples Test" in Figure 7.3), you will see "*t* Test for Equality of Means"— that's us. Back to the left of the output screen, you will notice "Equal variances assumed" and "Equal variances not assumed." For our work, we will disregard the row, "Equal variances not assumed," because we suspect that our variances within each university class *are* the same or similar. SPSS uses a procedure called "pooled variance estimate" to combine the two sample variances to obtain the most accurate estimate of the variance common to both classes.

Our observed *t* value of the comparison of our two university classes is 2.123, with degrees of freedom ($n - 1$ for each of the two groups) equal to 38. The two-tailed probability of .04 is less than our previously selected criteria of .05, which allows us to consider the difference significant and allows us to accept our hypothesis of a difference between our two university classes.

Excel

Since I am using both Excel and SPSS, and sometimes the terminology is different, I have placed simulated movies of both on the schoolsanddata.org Web site. First, be aware that Excel uses the words *two-sample* and SPSS uses *independent samples.* Enter University A's scores in Column A and University B's scores in Column B. Select **Tools,** then **Data Analysis,** and choose **t-Test: Two Samples Assuming Equal Variances.** Enter the data ranges, leave the hypothesized mean difference at 0, and the alpha level at .05. Click **OK**.

The Excel output reports both one- and two-tailed *p* values— we want to look at the two-tailed figure. We also need to look at both the *t* value and the *p* value to make a decision. In this case, the observed *t* value of the comparison of our two university

Figure 7.3   SPSS *t*-Test Printout

Group Statistics

		N	Mean	Std. Deviation	Std. Error Mean
exam	1	20	83.65	8.242	1.843
	2	20	77.25	10.672	2.386

Independent Samples Test

		Levene's Test for Equality of Variances		t Test for Equality of Means						95% Confidence Interval of the Difference	
		F	Sig.	t	df	Sig. (2-tailed)	Mean Difference	Std. Error Difference		Lower	Upper
exam	Equal variances assumed	3.747	.060	2.123	38	.040	6.400	3.015		.296	12.504
	Equal variances not assumed			2.123	35.718	.041	6.400	3.015		.284	12.516

95

classes is 2.123, with degrees of freedom ($n-1$ for each of the two groups) equal to 38. The two-tailed probability of .04 is less than our previously selected criteria of .05, which allows us to consider the difference significant and allows us to accept our hypothesis of a difference between our two university classes.

OK, YOUR TURN NOW

Let's try another example more closely related to your role as an educator. All of us continue to struggle with the problems of the limited-English speaker in our schools as languages other than English spoken in our schools continue to increase. My friend and colleague Ed is a principal in an elementary school in the Huntington Beach School District (California). His district administrators feel so strongly about offering English as a second language (ESL) as a way of helping the limited-English speaker adapt that they designated Ed's elementary school as a magnet school for K–3 students who speak English as a second language.

Ed is interested in determining if students in his school become English proficient better and faster than limited-English speakers in the general population of his district. He decides to compare a sample of third graders from his school with a sample of third graders (also limited-English speakers) from other schools in his district where ESL is not used as an instructional strategy. As best as can be determined, his samples account for such factors as similar number of years spent in public schools, and he assumes that the students in both samples have similar characteristics in other ways too. Both samples are given an English proficiency assessment measuring reading ability. Table 7.2 displays scores from both groups.

Using the data shown in Table 7.2, create a file in either SPSS or Excel titled "ESL Sample." You can view simulations for each procedure on the *Schools and Data* Web site at: http://www.schools anddata.org. They are posted under Chapter 7—The Independent-Samples *t* Test. Let's investigate whether or not there is a significant effect of ESL instruction (as measured by the proficiency test) with third grade limited-English students in Ed's school, when compared to students not receiving ESL instruction.

In setting up your file, let's code Ed's students as 1 and the other students as 2 (remember, SPSS and Excel don't understand

Table 7.2   Reading Scores of Students With and Without English as a Second Language (ESL) Program

Student	ESL	Student	No ESL
1	35	11	29
2	29	12	26
3	37	13	35
4	32	14	32
5	21	15	20
6	28	16	25
7	35	17	30
8	32	18	29
9	31	19	22
10	30	20	24

words—we must assign a number to each group). Use the independent-samples *t* test to test the null hypothesis that there is no difference in the mean scores between students receiving ESL instruction and those who do not. Use the .05 level of significance. Obviously, Ed's research hypothesis is that there is a statistical significant difference between the two groups.

Take a well-deserved break from my writing, and test your computer skills with either SPSS or Excel. Come back in a few minutes, and we will discuss Ed's findings.

Break's Over—How Did Ed's Students Do?

First of all, we notice from our data analysis that Ed's students had a mean score of 31 and the district's group attained a mean of 27.2. In essence, our question is, Is the mean difference great or different enough to allow us to reject the null hypothesis of no significant difference and in turn accept Ed's research hypothesis that ESL instruction has a positive effect on the acquisition of English proficiency skills?

Looking at our independent-samples *t* test analysis, we find an observed *t* value of 1.85 with a two-tailed probability (alpha level) of .08. We have a couple of problems here: (1) the observed *t* value of 1.85 is not as great as the critical t value of 2.10 that we find in Resource B (looking at .05 and 18 df), and (2) the alpha level of .08 indicates more possibility of error than our selected .05 criteria. The t test is not considered significant at the .05 level, so we must accept the null hypothesis of no significant difference in scores and reject Ed's research hypothesis. Figure 7.4 displays the test results.

Follow-Through

We should not leave Ed's hypothesis so quickly. Remember, statistical analysis does not prove anything; rather, it helps us identify patterns and encourages us to ask additional questions. Responsible data or evidence-based decision making involves looking beyond or below the surface for the real answers. Ed decides to look further at his two samples and discovers that there may be other variables at play here. Ed decides to do another study.

His suspicion now is that class size may be the influencing factor—in other words, he found he was comparing ESL instruction in classes of 30 with non-ESL instruction in classes of 20. He still believes ESL instruction is effective, but he also realizes that to really study the difference, he needs to control for class size. His new study will again look at ESL versus non-ESL instruction but, in addition, will compare three different class sizes (small, medium, and large).

CONCLUSION

As powerful as the t statistic is, it has one very obvious limitation. The t test can be used with only one or two samples or treatments. Ed's new questions involve the comparison of more than two sample means—six to be specific. He will have three sample means for ESL instruction (small, medium, and large) and three more sample means for non-ESL instruction (small, medium, and large).

We now need the help of something called *analysis of variance* (ANOVA). Wait a minute—don't leave me yet. The ANOVA sounds more complex and complicated than it really is. I promise it is no more intimidating than our work with Z scores a few chapters ago. Quite honestly, we are on the downhill side. Let's press on!

Figure 7.4 SPSS ESL Printout

Group Statistics

		N	Mean	Std. Deviation	Std. Error Mean
scores	1	10	31.00	4.522	1.430
	2	10	27.20	4.638	1.467

Independent-Samples Test

		Levene's Test for Equality of Variances		t Test for Equality of Means						95% Confidence Interval of the Difference	
		F	Sig.	t	df	Sig. (2-tailed)	Mean Difference	Std. Error Difference		Lower	Upper
scores	Equal variances assumed	.248	.625	1.855	18	.080	3.800	2.048		-.503	8.103
	Equal variances not assumed			1.855	17.988	.080	3.800	2.048		-.504	8.104

APPLICATION ACTIVITY

A high school math teacher feels strongly that students can learn math better outside of the classroom with hands-on materials and problems. He devises a semester course taught outside and integrating such tools as computer probeware, tape measures, thermometers, and measuring wheels. He is interested in determining the effect of this new course. His hypothesis is that the students taking the outdoor course will perform better than a class taught inside with the traditional instructional delivery, as measured by the annual standardized math achievement test administered by the district. The test scores of 10 students receiving outside instruction and the test scores of 10 students receiving inside instruction are listed in Table 7.3 (note that 1 = outside class and 2 = inside class).

We are testing the research hypothesis that there is a statistically significant difference in student math achievement as a result of outside hands-on instruction when compared to inside traditional instruction. Using either SPSS or Excel, create a data file with the information in Table 7.3. Conduct an independent-samples t test at the .05 level of significance. Don't forget degrees of freedom. (If you need help, the simulated procedure is available at: http://www.schoolsanddata.org.)

Table 7.3   Student Test Results

Student	Instruction	Score	Student	Instruction	Score
1	1	230	11	2	232
2	1	228	12	2	222
3	1	234	13	2	210
4	1	212	14	2	190
5	1	199	15	2	205
6	1	220	16	2	205
7	1	210	17	2	195
8	1	205	18	2	189
9	1	200	19	2	209
10	1	220	20	2	205

NCLB ACTIVITY

We are well aware that one of the mandates of No Child Left Behind (NCLB) states that a school (and district) is expected to make "adequate yearly progress" (AYP) toward the goal of 100% of students meeting state standards by the 2013–2014 school year. Your superintendent has asked you to investigate whether the sixth graders in your school are performing any better on their reading test scores this year compared to last year. Realizing that such a comparison would involve comparing two separate groups of students, you nonetheless want to see what is happening— since, in fact, your school's sixth grade scores will be compared in this way. Using what we have learned about the independent-samples t test, how would you set up such an investigation? Since you have these scores on record, it should be pretty easy to conduct such an investigation and have the requested information to your superintendent in a day or so.

CHAPTER EIGHT

Analysis of Variance

The Difference Between
Two or More Sample Means

A nalysis of variance (ANOVA) is a procedure for evaluating the mean difference between two or more samples. Yes, if you are looking at two means, you can use either the *t* test or the ANOVA—the result will be the same. But, with more than two samples or means, you *must* use the ANOVA. But wait a minute! Why can't we just use several *t* tests to analyze several means— you know, separate *t* tests for each pair of two samples. *Ah!* That's the problem. Let me see if I can convince you. Remember that each time we conduct a test, we set the alpha level at .05. In other words, we will accept that level of risk of error. Can you see if we conduct several *t* tests, that each time we would run the risk of .05 error? And if we conduct two *t* tests, we would actually double the error (that is, .05 plus .05). Yikes—that's .10 now. And if we conducted three *t* tests, we would actually triple the risk of error (that is, .05 plus .05 plus .05) and then have an inflated alpha level of .15. The cool thing about ANOVA is that it is only one operation (instead of several *t* tests), and it allows us to keep the alpha level at a safe .05 level. But in a sense, the *t* test and the ANOVA are quite similar. Both tests use sample data to test hypotheses about population means.

ADVANTAGES OF **ANOVA** OVER *t* TESTS

As stated before, the real advantage of ANOVA is the fact that it allows you to analyze two *or more* samples or treatments. A *t* test is an appropriate procedure for one or two samples, but not more than two. The ANOVA permits the educator to compare many variables at one time, allowing for much more flexibility. For instance, look at the information displayed in Table 8.1. In this example, we are interested in looking at the effect of two treatments: phonics versus whole language instruction. An additional question is, Are there differences across Schools A, B, and C?

Another very important advantage of the ANOVA has to do with our old friend, Type 1 error. Recall that when we set up our *t* test, we set an alpha level of .05—meaning that we expected (and would tolerate) a 1 in 20 chance of error in our test findings. For a moment, suppose we use the *t* test to analyze the data in Table 8.1. We would have to run individual *t* tests for each comparison of means (for example, between Sample 1 and Sample 2; between Sample 1 and Sample 3; and so on). You see the many different combinations required to cover all the pairings. Here's the problem: a probability error (.05) accompanies each individual test. You can see that if we only made six comparisons of means, we would run a .05 chance of error six times, causing the chance of error to rise dramatically. The ANOVA uses one test, with only one alpha level to analyze the mean differences, reducing significantly the possibility of making a Type 1 error.

Before we leave our data in Table 8.1, allow me to pose some hypothetical questions related to data-driven and evidence-based decision making. Suppose we found that in each of the three schools (A, B, C), there was a significant difference (as measured

Table 8.1   Introduction to ANOVA

	School A	*School B*	*School C*
Phonics Instruction	Sample 1	Sample 3	Sample 5
Whole Language Instruction	Sample 2	Sample 4	Sample 6

by a standardized test) between phonics and whole language instruction. Would it not be our professional and moral responsibility to closely scrutinize student achievement, instructional strategies, and assessment procedures? I believe so. Data analysis should be the basis for sound educational decision making.

USING THE ANALYSIS OF VARIANCE

Let's start off with what seems to be an oxymoron or contradiction in terms. The formulas and calculations necessary in the ANOVA are quite complicated—but conceptually, the ANOVA is pretty simple. Wow! Got that off my chest.

First of all, take a look at the data displayed in Table 8.2. I have kept the numbers small to help with understanding and conceptualization. Essentially, we are testing the null hypothesis that states there is no difference in the level of computer literacy among three different sizes of computer class (that is, small = 5–13 students; medium = 14–22 students; large = 23–30 students). A sample of five students was taken from each of the three different classes. The scores (dependent variable) represent the results of a computer competency test given to all three groups after two semesters of instruction.

Table 8.2   Computer Competency Scores for Samples of Students From Three Different-Sized Classes

Student	Class Size 2 (Small, 5–13 Students)	Class Size 1 (Medium, 14–22 Students)	Class Size 3 (Large, 23–30 Students)
1	5	2	1
2	4	2	2
3	5	2	1
4	3	1	1
5	3	3	2
	Mean = 4	Mean = 2	Mean = 1.4

At first, we notice a difference favoring the small class size. But remember, our goal is to find out if the difference is significant. Perhaps it just occurred by chance. The ANOVA will help us evaluate the difference—not the reason why, only whether there is a difference and whether it is statistically significant.

A Couple of New Terms

Before we proceed further with the ANOVA of our computer class size samples, I must introduce you to something called the F ratio. For ANOVA, the test statistic is called an F ratio as opposed to the t statistic discussed in earlier chapters. A procedural analysis of the F ratio and the t statistic may help.

$$t = \frac{\text{difference between sample means}}{\text{standard error}}$$

$$F = \frac{\text{variance between sample means}}{\text{variance of the standard error}}$$

You first notice that the F ratio uses the variance instead of the difference between sample means. There is a simple reason for this. Suppose you have two sample means: 22 and 32. Computing a sample mean difference is straightforward and easy to describe. However, suppose you have three sample means: 22, 32, and 41. Now describing the difference becomes more difficult, and there is really no way to calculate it. Using the variance to describe our three sample means is much easier—the reason for the ANOVA.

A confusion to most of us involves understanding that even though the F ratio uses the variance in the calculation, it is used to help us evaluate the differences in the means among samples, treatments, and population. The point is that both the t test and the ANOVA use sample data to test hypotheses about population means. To get there, the ANOVA uses the variance in calculation.

One other term needing clarification is *mean square* or *MS*. This one is easy too—it is a term that takes the place of the variance. In statistical circles, it is common to use the term *MS* instead of *variance*, but they are the same thing. You may remember the term *sum of squares (SS)*, which defines the sum of squared deviations. We now use *mean square (MS)* to distinguish the mean of the squared deviations. This becomes important as we read the SPSS and Excel report tables. More on this later.

Components of the ANOVA

Remember, the ANOVA measures the total amount of variability or variance. This total is composed of (1) the variance between the samples and (2) the variance within each individual sample. Reflect back for a moment to our data in Table 8.2. There is variance (and risk of error) across each of our class sizes. There is also variance (and risk of error) among the individual student scores within each of the three samples.

As promised, I will not elaborate on the complexity of the ANOVA formulas, but I cannot resist showing you the formula in words.

$$F = \frac{\text{variance between samples (treatments)}}{\text{variance within samples (treatments)}}$$

The *F* Distribution

In analysis of variance, the *F* ratio is exactly that—a ratio. The numerator in the ratio measures the variance between groups (samples), and the denominator measures variance within each of the groups (individual scores). An *F* distribution table appears in Resource C at the end of the book. The neat thing about this distribution table is that we do not have to concern ourselves with negative numbers. Think for a moment. Let's suppose that the null hypothesis is true—there is no difference in the variance. For that to be true, both the numerator and denominator would approximate the same number and result in something like 1/1. If *F* values approximate 1, the null hypothesis must be accepted (no difference). So, the *F* distribution table does not go below zero, and all values are positive. Figure 8.1 may help clarify. The distribution stops at 0, is highest around 1, and then tapers off to the right.

Figure 8.1   Distribution Curve of *F* Values

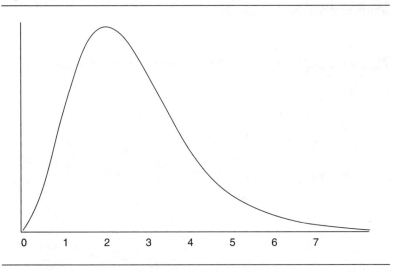

To use the *F* distribution table (Resource C), we must first be aware that we have two degrees of freedom: one for between groups and one for within groups. In our example of computer class size, our degrees of freedom (*df*) for between groups is 2 (3 classes − 1 class) and our degrees of freedom (*df*) for within groups is 12 (15 students − 3 students). Recall that we must subtract one student from each of the three samples because they are independent of each other and are being treated alone. It is important to repeat here that we are not discarding any samples or individual student scores. Though we are reducing a group by one, we still include that score in the sample. We are only reducing the number that is used in the calculation of the formula—this in essence is controlling for the risk of potential error. By reducing a number by one, we are increasing the likelihood that our decision will be correct.

We begin looking at the *F* distribution table by locating the number of degrees of freedom between groups (numerator) and then move down the column to find the number of degrees of freedom within groups (denominator). At this point, we find the critical value of *F* required to reject the null hypothesis of no difference between the variances. Resource C displays only the common alpha level of .05. But in Figure 8.2, I show you critical values for the alpha levels of both .05 and .01.

Figure 8.2   *F* Distribution With .05 and .01 Critical Regions

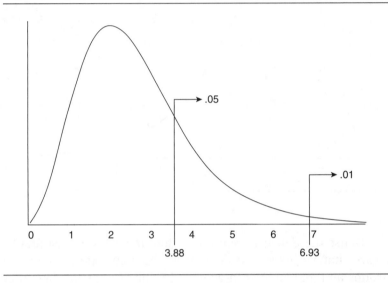

Sometimes we want to use .01 to test our data if we want a more powerful test result. You will notice two critical values: (1) 3.88 and (2) 6.93. The first is the critical value if we choose an alpha level of .05 and the second is the critical value if we selected .01 as an alpha level. Keep in mind that Figure 8.2 is based on our degrees of freedom (2, 12). (*Note:* The critical values will change depending on the number of groups we are investigating and the number of individual scores within each of our groups.)

As you can see, the critical value required (for .05) to reject the null hypothesis of no difference is 3.88. Any value resulting in our ANOVA test of 3.88 or higher gives us reason to reject the null and accept our research hypothesis that there is a statistical significant difference between the means of our three classes. Do you see why the critical value is 6.93 for an alpha level of .01?

We have arrived at another one of those "trusting moments." You must trust that my calculated *F* ratio for the computer class size test of 15.44 is correct and well beyond the critical value of 3.88, and that it meets the .01 level of significance. In this instance, I would have evidence (and confidence) to state a "large effect size" and "strong power" decision.

OK, let's put SPSS and Excel to the test. I am assuming you have created a file for our class size data that was displayed in Table 8.2. I will detail both software procedures, though they are pretty much alike in process. As in each chapter, these procedures can be found on the simulations link on the *Schools and Data* Web site at: http://www.schoolsanddata.org. First, SPSS.

SPSS

Insert the three class sizes in the first column, labeling with 1 for "small," 2 for "medium," and 3 for "large." These will be treated as subsets for one column. Select **Analyze,** then **Compare Means,** and finally **One-Way ANOVA.** You will be asked to choose a dependent variable (test scores) and a factor or independent variable (class size). The independent variable is the one that is manipulated or changed. Do you see how we are manipulating class size? We are setting three separate conditions (class size) in which to apply our treatment (computer instruction).

Please take note of a button labeled **Post Hoc**—just note the location, because we will come back to this in a moment. After selecting your dependent variable and your factor (independent), select **OK.** The SPSS ANOVA summary table is displayed in Figure 8.3.

You notice, SPSS displays the sum of squares, degrees of freedom, and mean squares. Again, the *F* ratio is 15.44 with a significance level of .000. Keep in mind that .000 is not really a level of zero—SPSS rounds off to three decimals. So this really means that the probability level is .0004 or less, rounded to .000. But

Figure 8.3   Output for SPSS ANOVA

ANOVA

	Sum of Squares	df	Mean Square	F	Sig.
Between Groups	18.533	2	9.267	15.444	.000
Within Groups	7.200	12	.600		
Total	25.733	14			

certainly and with confidence we can report $p < .05$, and to high-light power, $p < .001$ with a large effect size.

The observed F value of 15.44 is well beyond the critical region and above and beyond the required 3.88 at the .05 level of significance. Therefore, we reject the null hypothesis of no differ-ence and accept our research hypothesis of significant difference among our three class sizes.

Note that SPSS will also report descriptive statistics such as means and standard deviations—simply select **Options** from the screen that asks for the dependent variable and factor.

Excel

The procedure for setting up an ANOVA is very similar in Excel but differs in how you enter the data. We will not need to code the class sizes 1, 2, and 3. Just put your data in three separate columns—enter scores for small class size in Column A, scores for medium class size in Column B, and scores for large class size in Column C.

Select **Tools**, then **Data Analysis**, and choose **Anova: Single Factor**. Enter the data range for the three columns—remember to simply highlight with your mouse the three columns. Be sure your alpha level is set at .05 and select **OK**. The report, shown in Figure 8.4, reveals the same result as SPSS—an F value of 15.44444, and $p = .00048$. Excel obviously displays five decimals, so you see how we might round the 4 to 5 and conclude a p value of .0005, and state further $p < .001$. Pretty powerful, huh? See the simula-tion on the Web site at: http://www.schoolsanddata.org if you are unsure of the procedure or your findings.

A Note About Effect Size and Power

As we saw with the use of the t test, significant differences may only be trivial differences—it is important to examine a sig-nificant difference and determine if it is meaningful or important. And we really want to see if our finding is powerful. Stay with me—this involves a formula, but is already reported on our SPSS and Excel report. The effect size for ANOVA is calculated as some-thing we call "eta square" and is equal to: The sum of squares between groups divided by sum of squares total.

Figure 8.4   Excel ANOVA Results

	A	B	C	D	E	F	G
1	Anova: Single Factor						
2							
3	SUMMARY						
4	*Groups*	*Count*	*Sum*	*Average*	*Variance*		
5	Class Size 1	5	20	4	1		
6	Class Size 2	5	10	2	0.5		
7	Class Size 3	5	7	1.4	0.3		
8							
9							
10	ANOVA						
11	*Source of Variation*	*SS*	*df*	*MS*	*F*	*P-value*	*F crit*
12	Between Groups	18.53333	2	9.266667	15.44444	0.00048	3.885294
13	Within Groups	7.2	12	0.6			
14							
15	Total	25.73333	14				
16							

Values of .01, .06, and .14 represent small, medium, and large effects. Looking back at our SPSS or Excel report, we see sum of squares between groups being 18 and total sum of squares as 25. So, 18 divided by 25 equals .70—which is considered to be a strong effect. Essentially this means that the effect of class size on student achievement related to computer skills is great—good news for us and a pretty powerful finding.

Post Hoc Tests

So far, so good. Or is it? We feel confident in rejecting the null hypothesis of no difference because of the evidence that there is truly a significant difference across our three computer classes. So we accepted our research hypothesis of a significant difference across our three classes. Don't we really want to know *which* classes were different? At this point, we do not know if the smaller class size or the larger class size was more responsible for the difference. We might suspect the smaller, but we really do not know that with the ANOVA results. It is not unusual for the results of an analysis to create more questions than it answers.

The results of the ANOVA did not specify which class size was most different. Is there more difference between Class Size #1 and Class Size #2 or between Class Size #2 and Class Size #3? Or are #1 and #3 perhaps similar? Post hoc tests help us answer these types of questions.

When we were using the t test, there was no difficulty deciding where the difference was—it had to be between Sample 1 and Sample 2. Obviously, there was no need for a post hoc test. However, with the ANOVA (more than two samples), it is difficult to know for sure which means are different.

A post hoc test can be applied to the data after the ANOVA results are calculated. However, if the evidence supports the acceptance of the null hypothesis (no significant difference), then there is no need to even consider the post hoc procedure. It is only used if there is a significant difference reported in the ANOVA. In our class size example, there is a significant difference reported—and I suggest we really want to know if the difference is more related to the smaller computer classes as opposed to the larger ones.

One of the most common post hoc tests is Tukey's HSD test. The procedure computes a single value that is related to the two specific samples or treatments. This value is called the *honestly significant difference*. Let's look at the Tukey HSD test to determine exactly where the difference is in our class size ANOVA. Table 8.3 displays the SPSS Tukey test results.

Table 8.3   Tukey HSD Test for Class Size and Computer Proficiency Scores

Class Size	Class Size	Mean Difference	Significance
1	2	2.00*	.004
	3	2.60*	.001
2	1	−2.00*	.004
	3	.60	.462
3	1	−2.60*	.001
	2	−.60	.462

The Tukey HSD test reveals the most significant mean difference between Class Size #1 and Class Size #3 (2.60), and at a very significant alpha level of .001. No significant difference exists between Class Size #2 and Class Size #3 (.60) and at an unacceptable alpha level (.462). This gives us strong evidence and reason to suspect that something is happening between our smaller class size and our larger class size. Again, no cause and effect—but reason enough for further investigation and study.

CONCLUSION

In our class size analysis, we found that a very significant difference existed between our small class size and our large class size. Though the difference between our medium class size and large class size was not so great, a pattern was revealed, leading us to suspect that students' acquisition of computer skills increased as class size was reduced. Perhaps this is not earth shattering, but think for a moment about how we generally use computers in our schools. My experience shows that most districts put their time, effort, and monies into the construction of big, fancy computer labs. We then fill them up with large classes.

As many districts are discovering, perhaps the better way to use computers is to dismantle the computer labs and distribute the computers out to the individual classrooms. Much evidence has surfaced indicating that the optimum environment for computer instruction is three to five computers per classroom. As grand and impressive as computer labs are, they just may not be the best way to improve student achievement in computer skills or other areas of the curriculum. I hope you see how the simple one-way ANOVA can be used to help with the many decisions we must make regarding curriculum, student achievement, and assessment.

APPLICATION ACTIVITY

As director of curriculum for your district, you are interested in piloting three different language arts programs. Your plan is to test their use in three different classes over the next academic year. Set up a plan for conducting an analysis of variance (ANOVA) for the three programs, with the goal of determining if either is more effective than the others. And don't forget the post hoc procedure.

NCLB Activity

To help schools and districts meet the goals of No Child Left Behind (NCLB), the law provides a blend of requirements. One such requirement emphasizes aggregate and disaggregate analysis in the reporting of student achievement results. We certainly would be remiss if we did not investigate how our three ethnic groups (White, Black, and Hispanic) are performing on our state assessment instrument. Let's first look specifically at the area of mathematics.

Using an analysis of variance, let's investigate how our three ethnic groups did last year on the math portion of our state assessment. Input their scores into either SPSS or Excel, with each group in a separate column. Conduct an ANOVA to determine if any significant difference exists among our three groups.

You might also want to look at one specific group over a three-year period—get it? We could use the ANOVA to compare means from each of three different years of just one group. By using three years' scores, we are setting up a same kind of situation—three separate mean scores, and certainly we could use ANOVA here too.

CHAPTER NINE

Analysis of Variance

Repeated Measures

I n the previous chapter, we learned how to use analysis of variance (ANOVA) to compare the means across three groups (that is, small, medium, and large class sizes). You recall that we used a computer assessment as the dependent variable (not manipulated) that we administered to all in the three groups. The independent variable (manipulated) was the separate class sizes. As you get more and more involved with using data collection and analysis to improve your decision making in your school, you will begin to ask questions that involve other ways of using ANOVA.

In our class size example, we set up our analysis with a single factor (one independent variable), which was the three different class sizes. We also used an independent measures ANOVA because we used separate samples from each of the class sizes. In this chapter, we learn how to use the ANOVA for repeated measures—the same set of students analyzed three different times or in three different treatment situations. This technique is called *repeated measures analysis of variance.*

LET'S GET RIGHT TO AN EXAMPLE

When I was working as a sixth grade teacher for the Los Angeles Unified School District in the early 1980s, the Los Angeles Police Department implemented the now famous and nationally recognized

D.A.R.E. program. As you know, the program's purpose is to educate students about the dangers of drugs, alcohol, tobacco, and gang violence.

As teachers and administrators, we were pretty convinced that students' attitudes toward drugs and alcohol changed for the better during their sixth grade year when they were involved in the D.A.R.E. program. But our real question and concern was, Did students begin to revert back to their prior attitudes after the D.A.R.E. experience? In other words, could we determine if the positive effects of the program were short or long term? Did students tend to revert back to their negative attitudes as they moved up into the junior high grades?

We administered a student attitudinal survey to a fifth grade class to get an idea of their attitudes and beliefs before the D.A.R.E. involvement. We administered a similar attitudinal survey to the same class one year later, after their completion of the D.A.R.E. program. Finally, we administered the survey to the same students after their completion of seventh grade—1 full year after they received the D.A.R.E. instruction. Table 9.1 displays a set of data representing the class studied, along with their three separate attitudinal survey results.

The attitudinal survey consisted of 20 questions or statements that students responded to by answering on a Likert scale format (for example, with options ranging from 1 = *strongly disagree* to 4 = *strongly agree*). Ten of the items were phrased positively and 10 phrased negatively, avoiding the tendency for respondents to agree with positive statements regardless of their content. The range of possible scores was 20 (for all 1s) to 80 (for all 4s). The higher scores corresponded to a more positive attitude toward the dangers of drugs, alcohol, and gang violence. A sample statement was:

	1	*2*	*3*	*4*
	Strongly Disagree	Disagree	Agree	Strongly Agree
I believe smoking is wrong at school and home				

OK, let's see if the ANOVA can help us with our question of whether or not there might be a significant difference across these

Table 9.1   D.A.R.E. Attitudinal Survey Results

Student Number	Grade 5	Grade 6	Grade 7
1	54	62	56
2	57	62	52
3	44	56	45
4	46	58	48
5	55	60	58
6	54	65	56
7	57	62	52
8	44	58	45
9	46	60	48
10	55	62	58
11	54	65	56
12	57	62	52
13	44	54	45
14	46	55	48
15	55	62	52
16	54	65	56
17	57	62	52
18	44	58	45
19	46	60	48
20	55	62	58
21	54	65	56
22	57	62	52
23	44	50	45
24	46	58	48
25	55	62	58

three sets of responses. We have a *hunch* that might be the case. The purpose of the ANOVA is to compare the means in a statistical way to determine whether any difference exists; if so, we will use the Tukey test to locate specifically *where* the difference is. Let's review our four common steps for testing hypotheses or research questions:

1. State the hypothesis or research question and select an alpha level.

2. Decide on the degrees of freedom (*df*), and locate the critical region from the *F* distribution table in Resource C.

3. Compute the test statistic.

4. Make a decision regarding your hypothesis or research question (including a statement of effect size and power).

Step 1: State the Hypothesis or Research Question and Select an Alpha Level

Hypothesis: There is a statistically significant difference across the three years of student scores.

Research Question: Is there any significant difference across the three years of student scores?

Let's use the common alpha level of .05.

Step 2: Decide on the Degrees of Freedom and Locate the Critical Region

Remember, with the ANOVA, we have two different degrees of freedom: one *df* between groups and another *df* from within groups. This sounds a bit complicated, but just remember that we will have two numbers representing degrees of freedom—recall that the calculation is $N - 1$. The degrees of freedom between groups is pretty straightforward: $N - 1$ or $3 - 1$ (3 groups – 1 group) = 2 *df.* This is the number used in the numerator of the ANOVA division problem. OK, now the calculation of degrees of freedom for within groups is a bit more cumbersome, but it is really pretty simple—we will use $N - 1$ for each of the three groups and total. We have 25 students $(25 - 1)$, but we are assessing that group three times. So we need to calculate *df* for each of the three times and total. This gives us 72 $(25 - 1$ plus $25 - 1$ plus $25 - 1)$. Stating the degrees of freedom to check the critical region from Resource C we put the degrees of freedom for between groups (2) with the degrees of freedom for within groups (72). For the analysis, *df* equals (2, 72). Consulting the *F* distribution table in Resource C, we find that the critical region for 2, 72 is 3.10. Sometimes, as I will do in this example, we use a more stringent criteria to increase the power of our test. Though Resource C reveals 3.10 for *df* 2, 27, I will use the *df* for 2, 50 to increase the power of my ANOVA test. This means that the observed *F* value resulting from our ANOVA test must be 3.18 or greater for us to legitimately accept (at the alpha level of .05) our hypothesis of significant difference between our students' three-year responses.

Step 3: Compute the Test Statistic

Using SPSS or Excel, create a file using the data shown in Table 9.1. The easiest way to set up your SPSS file is to put your data in three separate columns—Column 1 for Grade 5 results, Column 2 for Grade 6 results, and Column 3 for Grade 7 results. There is no need for a coding variable. Figure 9.1 displays the D.A.R.E. data input screen.

Figure 9.1 D.A.R.E. Input for Repeated Measures ANOVA

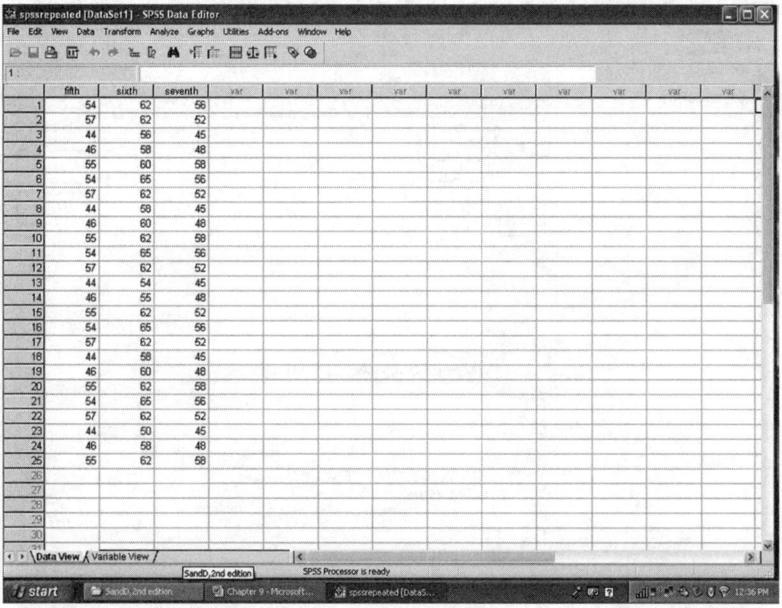

	fifth	sixth	seventh
1	54	62	56
2	57	62	52
3	44	56	45
4	46	58	48
5	55	60	58
6	54	65	56
7	57	62	52
8	44	58	45
9	46	60	48
10	55	62	58
11	54	65	56
12	57	62	52
13	44	54	45
14	46	55	48
15	55	62	52
16	54	65	56
17	57	62	52
18	44	58	45
19	46	60	48
20	55	62	58
21	54	65	56
22	57	62	52
23	44	50	45
24	46	58	48
25	55	62	58

To conduct an SPSS AVOVA using the repeated measures design, select **Analyze, General Linear Model,** then **Repeated Measures.** A **Define Factors** dialogue box will appear asking for a Within-Subject Factor Name—replace the word *factor1* with the word *grade.* Next, you have to tell SPSS how many levels there were to the variable (that is, how many testing conditions there were). In this case, there were three different testing times (Grades 6, 7, and 8), so we enter 3 in the box labeled "Number of Levels." Click on **Add** to add this variable to the list of repeated measures variables. Now, click on **Define** to go to the main dialogue box.

The main dialogue box (displayed in Figure 9.2) has a space entitled "Within-Subjects Variables" that contains a list of three question marks followed by a number. The question marks are for the variables representing the three levels of the independent variable.

To move the three variables, highlight each (or all three at once) and click the arrow button to transfer the three variables to the box replacing the question marks.

Figure 9.2   Main Dialogue Box for Repeated Measures ANOVA

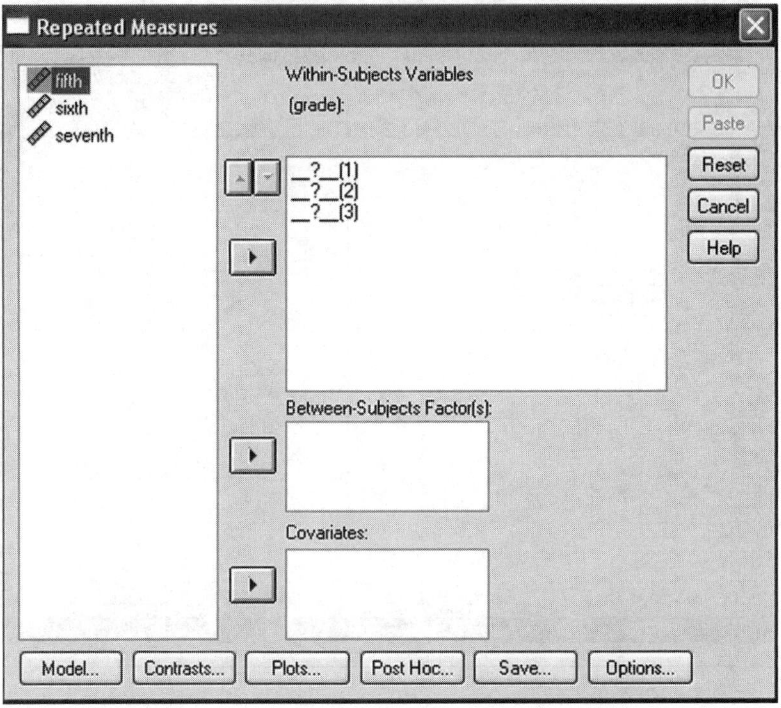

Now, stay with me, it gets a little tricky here. Note the two buttons at the bottom of the screen, **Options** and **Post Hoc**. After selecting **Options,** another dialogue box opens, and we want to move *grades* to **Display Means.** We also want to click on **Descriptive** while we are there, and be sure to select **Compare Main Effects,** since this is really the most important component of an ANOVA. Then, select one of the post hoc tests from the drop-down menu— let's choose the **Bonferroni method**. Remember from Chapter 8, on one-way ANOVA, we need a post hoc test to help us locate the specific difference. Then click **Continue,** taking you back to the main dialogue box, and click on **OK.** The Repeated Measures ANOVA results appear.

Step 4: Make a Decision Regarding Your Hypothesis or Research Question

To make a decision, we need some information from the ANOVA summary table as shown in Figure 9.3. The information we want is the F ratio and the probability (significance or alpha level). The value of F is 137.798, with a significance of .000 (remember SPSS rounds off to three decimal places), or less than .001. Wow! We can now conclude that there was a significant difference between the fifth, sixth, and seventh grade responses.

Figure 9.3   SPSS Repeated Measures Output

Tests of Within-Subjects Effects

Measure: MEASURE_1

Source		Type III Sum of Squares	df	Mean Square	F	Sig.
grade	Sphericity Assumed	1321.787	2	660.993	137.798	.000

However, this main ANOVA test does not tell us which responses were different—or exactly *where* the difference lies. Fortunately, we selected a post hoc test (Bonferroni) to help us identify any significant difference. In your SPSS output, you will notice a report entitled "Pairwise Comparisons." It is here that we can really zero in on where the difference is. Look closely at Figure 9.4 and we will see what occurred.

If you are using Excel, you will also want each year's responses in three separate columns. Rather than explain in detail here, I recommend that you visit the *Schools and Data* Web site at: http://www.schoolsanddata.org and view the data sets posted under Chapter 9: (1) D.A.R.E. SPSS and (2) D.A.R.E. Excel.

What About Effect Size?

The observed F ratio identifies the critical region as 137.80, way out in the distribution tail, well beyond the required 3.18 we calculated from Resource C (*df* 2, 12 at .05 alpha level). We should feel confident about the decision to accept our research hypothesis that there is a statistically significant difference across

Figure 9.4   SPSS Post Hoc Test

Pairwise Comparisons

Measure: MEASURE_1

(I) grade	(J) grade	Mean Difference (I-J)	Std. Error	Sig.[a]	95% Confidence Interval for Difference[a]	
					Lower Bound	Upper Bound
1	2	−9.080*	.666	.000	−10.793	−7.367
	3	−.360	.594	1.000	−1.889	1.169
2	1	9.080*	.666	.000	7.367	10.793
	3	8.720*	.596	.000	7.186	10.254
3	1	.360	.594	1.000	−1.169	1.889
	2	−8.720*	.596	.000	−10.254	−7.186

Based on estimated marginal means
* The mean difference is significant at the .05 level.
a. Adjustment for multiple comparisons: Bonferroni.

our three separate D.A.R.E. responses. *But,* let's look at the effect size to determine the power or importance of our decision. Recall that for the ANOVA, effect size is calculated by dividing the sum of squares between groups by the total sum of squares (1289/2878). And recall that levels of .01, .06, and .14 represent small, medium, and large effect sizes. Our result is .45, and can be considered a strong effect size, providing further evidence that the difference is pretty important. In addition, the resulting significance in our ANOVA test is less than .001 (remember, SPSS rounds to three decimals), giving us even further support for our position that the result did not just happen by chance.

ONE MORE QUESTION: WHERE DOES THE DIFFERENCE LIE?

Recall that the ANOVA tells us *only* that there is a significant difference. We really want to know if the difference is between the fifth and sixth grade responses, between sixth and seventh, or between fifth and seventh. Remember the post hoc tests? We will seek help from the Tukey procedure in identifying the exact location of the significant difference between means in our three sets of responses.

Probably you selected the Post Hoc option in the ANOVA procedure. If not, simply go back to the data file and run it again. Without getting too technical, the Tukey post hoc test measures the difference between the individual groups being compared in the ANOVA. As you see in Figure 9.5, the difference between the fifth grade scores and the sixth grade scores (1 and 2) is very significant at even the .01 alpha level. Looking more closely, we notice that the difference between the fifth grade and seventh grade scores is not that significant (−.60) with a very risky alpha level of .894—much larger than our selected .05 criteria. This implies that the scores of fifth and seventh are somewhat similar. Then, further, we see a very significant difference between the sixth grade scores and the seventh grade scores (2 and 3). What do you think is going on here? Hmmm . . . !

Figure 9.5   Tukey Post Hoc Procedure

Multiple Comparisons

Dependent Variable: TEST
Tukey HSD

(I) Students	(J) Students	Mean Difference (I–J)	Std. Error	Sig.	95% Confidence Interval	
					Lower Bound	Upper Bound
1	2	−9.08(*)	1.329	.000	−12.26	−5.90
	3	−.60	1.329	.894	−3.78	2.58
2	1	9.08(*)	1.329	.000	5.90	12.26
	3	8.48(*)	1.329	.000	5.30	11.66
3	1	.60	1.329	.894	−2.58	3.78
	2	−8.48(*)	1.329	.000	−11.66	−5.30

* The mean difference is significant at the .05 level.

SPSS provides one last comparison to help us with the interpretation of our findings. It is a test of *homogeneous subsets*. Essentially, the test places like means together and displays any means that are very different. Table 9.2 shows the report, revealing that Groups 1 and 3 are almost the same (51.2 and 51.8). Not very different, huh? But, Group 2 (sixth grade) is very different—aha!— now we are seeing something very important. The responses (means) changed drastically from fifth to sixth grade, *but* returned

Table 9.2   Homogeneous Subsets for D.A.R.E. Attitudinal Survey

	N	Subsets for Alpha = .05	
Student Group		1	2
1 (Grade 5)	25	51.20	
3 (Grade 7)	25	51.80	
2 (Grade 6)	25		60.28

to almost the same scores in seventh. In other words, the students' positive attitudes increased during the time of the D.A.R.E. curriculum and activities, but after a year later, in seventh grade, the attitudes seem to return to the level existing before the D.A.R.E. training.

CONCLUSION

We need to be careful that we do not create a *cause-and-effect* interpretation here. Some might argue that D.A.R.E. causes negative attitudes regarding drugs and alcohol because the student attitudes declined after the first year. No, not necessarily! Perhaps the results are due to other societal factors (junior high school environment, the transition from elementary to junior high, and so on). However, we are faced with the potential for some very constructive data-driven decision making.

The finding does not indicate that the D.A.R.E. program is ineffective, but it may indicate to us that the program must continue for more than one year. As you probably know, during the past several years, the D.A.R.E. program has expanded to both lower grades (fifth) and higher grades (seventh and eighth). Perhaps this is the reason—their studies revealed similar results to ours. In addition, we as educators may want to look very closely at our own curriculum and efforts. Perhaps there are some changes we can make to curb undesirable attitudes about drugs and alcohol at the junior and senior high school levels.

For those of you not familiar with the D.A.R.E. program, the contact time with the D.A.R.E. officer consists of 1 or 2 hours per week. I might suspect that this small amount of time might produce short-term attitudinal effects and that more contact time might produce more longer-term effects. So you see, the "culprit" may not be the D.A.R.E. program itself but the extremely limited amount of time spent on activities and instruction. An important point here: data analysis can be accomplished by the click of the mouse and software programs, but it is *interpretation* that is the essence of good research and providing us with information helpful in the solution of problems.

APPLICATION ACTIVITY

The dean and school board of education of the newly opened charter school in the district are interested to see if reading comprehension increases significantly over the course of the year in third grade. The state department of education administers a reading indicator assessment three times per year that measures three levels of reading comprehension: (1) above average = 1, (2) average = 2, and (3) below average = 3.

In other words, the charter school administration would like to know if there are statistically significant changes in reading comprehension across the three assessments. The following data represent a sample of 10 third graders from the school:

Student Number	1st Assessment	2nd Assessment	3rd Assessment
1	1	1	1
2	3	3	2
3	2	2	1
4	2	2	2
5	2	1	1
6	3	3	2
7	1	1	1
8	2	1	1
9	3	2	2
10	1	1	2

1. Compute the mean score for each assessment.

2. Use a repeated measures ANOVA to determine if there are significant differences among the three assessment periods. Use the .05 level of significance.

NCLB ACTIVITY

One of the goals of No Child Left Behind (NCLB) is to have "highly qualified teachers" in core academic subjects by 2005–2006. Certainly, most of a teacher's preparation takes place in his or her university preparation program, and in most states is measured by a state teachers' examination. Your local university administers a practice exam to their students three times before the actual test is taken upon teacher certification. Request a year's set of three practice exams, and use a repeated measures ANOVA to investigate any improvement in scores over the year. In other words, you want to see if any significant difference is occurring from Test 1 to Test 2, and from Test 2 to Test 3.

CHAPTER TEN

Two-Way Analysis of Variance

Two Independent Variables

Y ou're probably wondering! First he said that the Z score method could be used to test hypotheses, then he said the *t* test was better. As soon as we thought the end was in sight, he presented the *independent-samples ANOVA* and then continued with the *repeated measures ANOVA*. We thought we were near the end— now what is this thing called *two-way analysis of variance?*

First of all, I assure you that this is the last chapter dealing with the analysis of variance. Let me also assure you that if you feel pretty comfortable with the independent measures ANOVA (Chapter 8), you will breeze through this chapter on the two-way ANOVA. So, let's get on with it! What's the difference?

The basic strategies used in the one-way ANOVA apply as well to the two-way ANOVA. The statistic calculated in both is the *F* ratio. The *F* ratio serves the same purpose in the two-way ANOVA as it did in the one-way ANOVA: It helps us determine if the difference between means is different enough to be considered statistically significant or if it could have occurred by chance.

WORKING WITH TWO INDEPENDENT VARIABLES

Our discussion and examples up to this point have focused on studies that had one independent variable (for example, class size) and one dependent variable (for example, test or assessment). But in our school buildings and communities, variables rarely exist in such a neat fashion. More often, many different variables are interacting simultaneously. We saw in Chapter 9 that we suspect that the D.A.R.E. variable is not alone in influencing student attitudes. It is likely that other factors such as family life, school environment, and even gender take part in the creation of negative or positive attitudes toward drugs and alcohol.

The two-way ANOVA allows us to look at the effects and interactions of *two independent variables*. For example, we want to study student achievement in both cooperative learning and direct instruction situations. But we also want to look at courses using each of the two instructional strategies. Table 10.1 displays the structure of a study examining the instructional delivery versus class content areas.

Table 10.1   Two-Way ANOVA Matrix: Instructional Strategy by Content Area

	Math	*Reading*	*Science*
Cooperative Learning	Scores for 20 students in math with cooperative learning	Scores for 20 students in reading with cooperative learning	Scores for 20 students in science with cooperative learning
Direct Instruction	Scores for 20 students in math with direct instruction	Scores for 20 students in reading with direct instruction	Scores for 20 students in science with direct instruction

The first thing you probably notice is that the study involves separate samples of students rather than the same sample repeated. There are six different samples being tested, to be specific. Each cell in Table 10.1 contains a separate sample of students tested with the same dependent variable (standardized test). The two-way ANOVA allows us to test for mean differences across the six instructional situations.

You can guess what our questions might be. The research questions are pretty straightforward. Is direct instruction or cooperative learning a better strategy for teaching math, reading, and science? Is there any difference between the two instructional strategies? Does perhaps one strategy work better in math whereas another works better in science? We might find evidence to support the use of cooperative learning as an effective teaching strategy in all three content areas (main effect). If this were the case, there would be no interaction between the two instructional strategies. Let's suppose, however, we find that cooperative learning reveals higher student achievement in math, reading, and science, and that direct instruction reveals lower student achievement in the three content areas. Figure 10.1 shows *main effect* due to the type of instructional strategy.

Figure 10.1 Main Effect Due to Type of Instructional Strategy

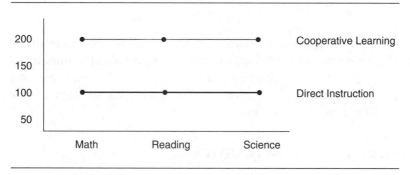

Figure 10.1 suggests that the two instructional strategies differ consistently in student achievement. The subject taught has no effect on student achievement with regard to the method of instruction. Slipping into statistical language for a moment, we observe a main effect due to the *instructional strategy* used in the classroom. We observe no main effect due to the *subject* taught.

Figure 10.2 displays an entirely different result. Often the independent variables overlap or interact. The data now reveal that cooperative learning seems to work well in math and science but perhaps not so well in reading. As you see, direct instruction seems to work better in reading but not so well in math and science. Interaction is occurring between instructional strategies and course content. Some combinations of instructional strategy and course taught result in higher student achievement than do other combinations. In Figure 10.2, we observe *interaction* between instructional strategy and content taught.

Figure 10.2 Interaction Between Instructional Strategy and Content

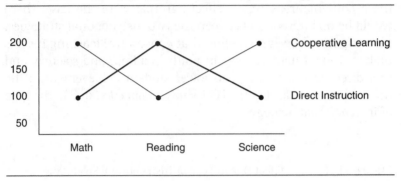

As you now see, the two-way ANOVA allows you to evaluate the *main effect* of each factor individually and also the amount of *interaction* between the two factors. Figure 10.2 shows only one possible example of interaction. You can readily see that a wide variety of results can occur.

Steps for the Two-Way ANOVA

The steps used in the two-way ANOVA are identical to the four steps we have been using all along for hypotheses testing.

1. State the research hypothesis or research question, and set an alpha level.

2. Locate the critical region required to accept the research hypothesis.

3. Compute the *F* ratios.

4. Make a decision regarding the hypothesis or research question.

We will stay with our cooperative learning and direct instruction sample and work through a two-way ANOVA. The two-way ANOVA helps us to investigate three separate research questions or hypotheses:

1. Is there a significant difference in student achievement across math, reading, and science?

2. Is there a significant difference between classes taught by cooperative learning and classes taught by direct instruction?

3. Is there any interaction between instructional strategy and course content?

Table 10.2 displays the total scores of six samples of students (five students in each) drawn from six different teaching situations: (1) math class/cooperative learning, (2) math class/direct instruction, (3) reading class/cooperative learning, (4) reading class/direct instruction, (5) science class/cooperative learning, and (6) science class/direct instruction.

Table 10.2   Test Data for Instructional Strategy and Content Area

Student Number	Math/ Cooperative Learning	Math/ Direct Instruction	Reading/ Cooperative Learning	Reading/ Direct Instruction	Science/ Cooperative Learning	Science/ Direct Instruction
1	260	220	220	265	260	220
2	248	230	225	250	245	230
3	250	235	235	255	255	230
4	255	225	230	246	250	240
5	245	240	240	250	255	220

Using the data from Table 10.2, create a file in either SPSS or Excel. Using Excel, simply place each of the six groups in each of six columns. For SPSS, put *all* the groups' scores in one column, and in an adjoining column, code each group with 1, 2, 3, 4, 5, or 6. As always, you are encouraged to visit the *Schools and Data* Web site at: http://www.schoolsanddata.org to review the simulated tutorials for both the SPSS and Excel procedures. Table 10.3 displays the mean scores for the six different content/instructional strategy combinations, as reported in Excel and SPSS.

It appears scores are lowest in three learning situations: (1) direct instruction in math, (2) cooperative learning in reading, and (3) direct instruction in science. Note that the mean scores decrease for cooperative learning in the reading class. For that same

Table 10.3   Mean Scores for the Content Area/Instructional Strategy
Combinations

	Math	Reading	Science
Cooperative Learning	251.6	230	253
Direct Instruction	230	253.2	228

class (reading), the highest scores represent direct instruction as a
more appropriate instructional strategy.

In addition to displaying the sample descriptive statistics, SPSS
and Excel produce an ANOVA summary table, as shown in Table
10.4. Hang on, this gets a bit technical, but we'll go slowly (and
remember, this procedure is posted at http://www.schoolsanddata
.org).

Table 10.4   ANOVA Summary Table

Source	Type III Sum of Squares	df	Mean Square	F	Sig.
Corrected Model	4080.967	5	816.193	15.473	.000
Intercept	1741948.033	1	1741948.033	33022.712	.000
SECTION	6.467	2	3.233	.061	.941
INSTRUCT	456.300	1	456.300	8.650	.007
SECTION* INSTRUCT	3618.200	2	1809.100	34.296	.000
Error	1266.000	24	52.750		
Total	1747295.000	30			
Corrected Total	5346.967	29			

$r^2 = .763$ (Adjusted $r^2 = .714$)

The F value for the model is very significant ($F = 15.473$,
$p < .001$), revealing that there are major differences between the
mean scores of our six groups (we don't know where yet). Looking
closer, we see no significant main effect for SECTION ($F = .061$,
$p > .05$), and some main effect for INSTRUCTION ($F = 8.6, p < .05$).
The important finding relates the *interaction* found between
SECTION and INSTRUCTION ($F = 34.29, p < .001$). We will see
more clearly what is happening by looking at Figure 10.3.

Figure 10.3 Interaction Between INSTRUCTION and SECTION

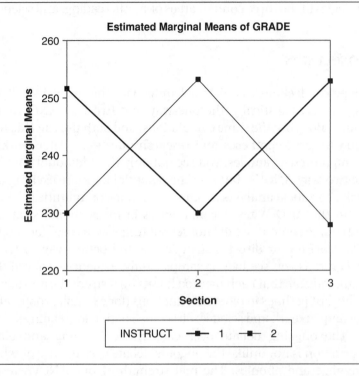

What we see here tells more of the story. Recall that Instruction 1 represents cooperative learning strategy and Instruction 2 represents direct instruction strategy. Sections 1, 2, and 3 represent math, reading, and science respectively. Look closely! Cooperative learning (Instruction 1) reveals higher mean scores in math and science, but significantly lower mean scores in reading. Direct instruction (Instruction 2) reveals lower mean scores in math and science, but significantly higher mean scores in reading.

What does this mean? Well, we will be careful about implying *cause and effect* here, but there is substantial evidence that although cooperative learning seems to work well as a strategy in math and science, it may not be the best strategy for reading (direct instruction results in higher scores). And conversely, though direct instruction seems to work well in the content area of reading, it may not be the best strategy for math and science classes.

The results of the ANOVA test provide significant evidence allowing us to accept our research hypothesis of significant difference between cooperative learning and direct instruction as instructional strategies in the three content areas of math, reading, and science.

CONCLUSION

I hope you feel more comfortable now with the two-way ANOVA. As you see, logistically, the one-way and two-way ANOVAs are similar. Both use the same calculations, and both use the F distribution to test hypotheses and research questions. After working through these examples, you see not only the additional power of the two-way ANOVA, but also the potential for more exciting and useful statistical analyses in our schools and communities.

In the ANOVA test for differences in instructional strategies and course content, we did not set out to "prove a case" for cooperative learning or direct instruction as the better way to teach. However, as you see by our sample study, evidence surfaced that might indicate that each method has its own strengths and applicability but perhaps in different situations (for example, cooperative learning in math and science; direct instruction for reading).

The ongoing debate over cooperative learning and direct instruction is not unlike the ongoing debate over the use of whole language and phonics. The real strength of our ANOVA test is perhaps the evidence that the two instructional strategies *interact* more than we sometimes think. To suggest to our teachers that they should use one or the other exclusively is a mistake. I have seen from my experience, and perhaps you have from yours, that our schools (and state and national departments of education) often use a decision-making process that's driven by a desire to select one method or strategy and reject the others. The examples abound: (1) either whole language or phonics, (2) either standardized tests or performance-based assessment, (3) either constructivism or back to basics, and (4) either ESL or English only. The lists goes on and on, doesn't it?

Too often, we do not recognize the strengths of several strategies in combination rather than one alone. Our ANOVA points to the value of using the instructional strategies of cooperative learning and direct instruction in combination. Collecting sound data and analyzing carefully and appropriately will assist us in our decision making as we educators are faced with an almost daily barrage of problems.

It is no secret that our profession is under careful scrutiny by our state and national legislators, communities, and yes, the universities. I cannot imagine a better time for us to consistently use data to improve decision making in our schools for the benefit of effective teaching and learning. Yes, it is hard work, time consuming, and sometimes costly. But what's our choice?

APPLICATION ACTIVITY

You are the principal of a large K–8 school district. Each year, the high school counselors come to your school and present a reading readiness lecture to all eighth graders for the purpose of placement in language arts courses at the high school. One week after the lecture, students are tested on the material covered in the lecture. *You are interested in knowing whether students perform any differently if they all attend the lecture in the auditorium rather than each class in their individual classrooms.* In addition, you are interested to see whether students score differently on the assessment instrument if they receive the test in the auditorium as opposed to the regular classroom. You arrange to have half of the eighth graders hear the lecture in the auditorium and the other half in their individual classrooms. Of the students hearing the lecture in the auditorium, half are tested in the same auditorium while the other half are tested in their classroom. Similarly, one half of the students hearing the lecture in the classroom are tested in the same classroom while the other half are tested in the auditorium. You end up with four groups of students with their test scores as shown in the table on page 136. The scores represent correct answers on the assessment instrument.

Using a two-way ANOVA, determine if the size of the lecture facility and/or the size of the testing facility have a statistically significant effect on the eighth graders' performance.

NCLB ACTIVITY

Clearly, one of NCLB's goals states that "all students will graduate from high school." Obviously, we are a long way from accomplishing this lofty goal, but you want to determine strategies for increasing the graduation rates in your district.

	Auditorium Testing	*Classroom Testing*
Auditorium Lecture	10	7
	12	9
	14	5
	10	8
	11	7
Classroom Lecture	5	12
	9	15
	8	12
	9	11
	10	10

You are aware that many factors influence graduation rates—socioeconomic status, educational background of parents, grade point average, participation in extracurricular activities, and several others. Set up a two-way ANOVA matrix that you might use as a beginning of a two-way ANOVA treatment. Graduation rates will be your dependent variable (what you want to measure), and you want to record rates for your three ethnic groups (Whites, Blacks, and Hispanics). In addition to determining whether there is any *main effect* between any of your ethnic groups, you also want to see whether there is any *interaction* between socioeconomic status. *Hint:* Your matrix should consist of six cells (3 × 2) that will represent six different mean graduate rate scores.

CHAPTER ELEVEN

What If No Mean Scores?

The Chi-Square Test for Goodness of Fit

I think you may know what's coming in this chapter. We have previously focused on tests of relationship (correlation) or tests for comparing means (*t* test and ANOVA). We have, up to this point, had a numerical score (for example, grade point average, math score, statistics exam score) for each individual in our sample. The statistics procedures (parametric) used with these *interval* data basically *add, square, average,* or otherwise manipulate the number.

In many cases, we educators are faced with situations for which we do not have interval data. For example, our district's graduation rate is based on a simple count turned into a percentage (for example, 75 out of 100 students graduated—a 75% graduate rate). Even our state's assessment and the No Child Left Behind (NCLB) requirements ask for the number of students who passed, not specific scores. So here, too, we have a measurement (percentage passed) based on simple counts rather than numerical scores. These kinds of data are called *nominal data*—and must be treated differently from interval data that results in means and variances. So, this chapter introduces a procedure for analyzing nominal data that is called a *nonparametric test*.

Stay with me for a moment—I want to make sure you are clear on our direction. OK, parametric/nonparametric; interval/nominal; but tell me exactly how they differ. Let's use a couple of examples. I want to investigate retention in kindergarten in my district. And I want to see if our retention rate (%) is similar to the state average of 5%. Why? Well, the board of education is considering a no-retention policy, and I need some data (evidence) to report to them and our community as we study this situation. I will simply "classify" students into two different categories—passed and retained. No interval-type number, and no "shades of gray." A child will either be a *pass* or a *retain*. As you see, a child can't be halfway between or an average of the two. So we have nominal data here—simply a name, frequency, or a count.

What I am really interested in determining here is whether our rate of retaining at kindergarten is any different from the state's average. And like our other tests, I am interested in *statistically significant difference.* And the good news is that there is a nonparametric test called "chi-square goodness of fit" that allows me to conduct the study with only nominal data.

One more example, before we move on. Recall from Chapters 1 and 2 that a frequency distribution is the tabulation of the number of individuals located in each category of the scale of measurement. With chi-square tests, we place the frequency (or counts) in a series of boxes, with each box representing a separate category in the scale. Figure 11.1 shows how this information is presented for a distribution for a set of $n = 48$ students.

Figure 11.1 Setting Up the Chi-Square Test for Goodness of Fit

f	White	Black	Hispanic
White 21			
Black 12	21	12	15
Hispanic 15			

Though there are several variations of the chi-square test, for the purposes of this chapter, we will focus on the most common, the chi-square test for goodness of fit. This test uses frequency counts from a sample and compares them to the frequency count of the population. In many cases, we know the *expected* frequency count from the population—for instance, we know from the literature and state department data that the number (average) of special education students in the population is approximately 10% of a district's total enrollment. This is the figure that state and national departments use as a guide and recommendation.

Let me specifically state the definition of the chi-square test of goodness of fit: *The test uses frequency counts from a sample and compares those counts to the expected frequency count from the population.* So, in this example, we would be interested in finding whether the frequency counts of special education students in our district are similar to (or different than) the *expected* frequency in the population (state and national estimates). The chi-square test will help us answer these questions. Table 11.1 shows some hypothetical data from our district compared to the state and national figure.

Table 11.1   Expected and Observed Frequencies of Special Education and Regular Students

	Special Ed (%)	*Regular Ed (%)*
Expected	10	90
Observed (sample)	22	78

You notice that the frequency of special education students in our sample is different than the expected frequency (that is, 22% versus 10%). Just as in the *t* test and the ANOVA, we want to determine whether the difference is "different enough" to be considered significant, or is it possible that the difference occurred by chance?

THE CHI-SQUARE FORMULA

I know, we are not supposed to be dealing with complex formulas in *Schools and Data*, but in this case I think it will help us conceptualize the procedure for chi-square.

$$\chi^2 = \sum \frac{(f_o - f_e)^2}{f_e}$$

First, the symbols. The chi-square statistic we are searching for is χ^2; f_o represents the observed frequency in our sample; f_e represents the expected frequency based on prior knowledge; and $\sum$ is the sign for summing. So, the chi-square statistic follows these steps:

1. Find the difference between our observed frequency (f_o) and the expected frequency (f_e) for each of the categories in separate boxes.

2. Square the difference for each (eliminating negative values and ensuring all will be positive).

3. Then, divide the squared difference by f_e for each of the categories.

4. Finally, sum the values from all the categories.

Conceptualize with me for a moment. The chi-square formula measures the discrepancy between the observed frequencies (sample) and the expected frequencies (population). When these differences are large, the chi-square value will be large and will conclude that our sample (observed) is not similar to the population (expected) and therefore can be considered statistically significantly different. If, on the other hand, the differences are small, and result in a "not different enough" situation, we conclude that there is not a statistically significant difference between our sample and the population.

Time Out!

You may say, "OK, I understand that we want to look at the difference between the observed and expected, but why do we divide by f_e?" We need an analysis to illustrate the need for dividing by f_e.

Pretend that we have scheduled a parent meeting and prepared refreshments for our *expected* 200 parents. But, since we have on the agenda a discussion of the end-of-year graduation party, we actually have 220 parents attend. Twenty more parents than expected should not cause a problem with enough refreshments. On the other hand, suppose we had 320 parents in attendance? *Yikes!* A hundred and twenty extra parents would be a problem, huh?

How significant the difference is depends in part on the number we were originally expecting. To correct for this error between f_o and f_e, we divide the squared differences for each category by its expected frequency. By doing this, the calculation of the chi-square value takes into account the possibility of large error between what is observed and what is expected.

OK, Let's Practice With a Real-Life Example

A few years ago, as superintendent of the Westside School District in California, I was discussing the food service with our cafeteria manager. We had just implemented a "salad bar" for our lunch menu. Students had a choice—either the day's regular menu or the salad bar. Though we had a general idea the salad bar was popular and worth the investment, we needed evidence that would help convince the board of trustees for its continued use. We also suspected that there were certain items on the regular menu that appealed to students (for example, hot dogs, hamburgers, and pizza). We were interested to see exactly *where* the salad bar fit into the larger picture.

A special note is required here. I will not suggest to you that as a building principal or superintendent, that you announce to your staff (or board) that you are going to conduct a statistical test to determine the future of the cafeteria salad bar. I am the first to admit that we need to be careful how we present data analysis to our clients (parents, teachers, students, and boards of trustees). My point is, if you talk to my former cafeteria manager today, she will have no knowledge of a "chi-square test of goodness of fit." The issue of *communication* in regard to statistical analyses is so important that I have devoted a section to communication later in this chapter. Enough for now!

Determining Expected Frequencies

To help us choose (or determine) our expected frequencies, we need to consider one of two options:

1. There are no preferred choices between or among our categories. For example, if we asked students to choose their favorite class between math and science, we would conjecture that the result would be an even response—50% for math and 50% for science. This is called a "no preference hypothesis."

2. There is evidence of a preferred distribution of choices among categories. For example, if we were investigating the number of special education students in our district, we already have an expected distribution of counts—90% regular education and 10% special education, as stated as the benchmark from the state and federal government.

For our study of the salad bar, we will use Option 1 above—we have no reason to suspect there will be any significant difference among our four choices: (1) salad bar, (2) hot dogs, (3) hamburgers, or (4) pizza. So, we will set up the following boxes for our chi-square test:

	Salad Bar	Hot Dogs	Hamburgers	Pizza
Observed				
Expected	1/4	1/4	1/4	1/4

Another Brief Time-Out

As you probably gather, I have a habit of waiting until the very last minute to throw another "Yes, but" response at you. Before we go any further, I want to revisit two components of most tests: (1) degrees of freedom and (2) critical region of the distribution. Remember in the t test and the ANOVA we needed to be aware of df (degrees of freedom), which essentially was $N-1$ for groups in the test. The cool thing about calculating df for chi-square is that you simply subtract 1 from the categories $(C-1)$. So, in our salad bar study, df will be 3 (4 categories minus 1).

OK, for the critical region. Just as in the t distribution and the F distribution, we determine a point at which we will decide significance (critical region). The chi-square is no exception to this requirement. But, alas! A chart is available (see Resource D). Just be aware that with the chi-square statistic, df is based not on the size of the sample, but on the number of categories.

You're Still With Me?
Let's Get Back to the Cafeteria

Yep, we have steps again to follow.

Step 1. The Hypothesis Is Stated and a Significance Level Selected

Let's try this.

Since we have no evidence to think otherwise, the students of Westside School will show no preference of any of our four menu choices. So, we have the following expected frequencies:

Salad Bar	Hot Dogs	Hamburgers	Pizza
1/4	1/4	1/4	1/4

We will set the significance (alpha level or chance of Type 1 error) at .05.

Step 2. Determine the Degrees of Freedom (*df*) and Locate the Critical Region

Yes, I am going to go through this, but remember, SPSS and Excel will automatically do this for us. Checking Resource D, we find that for *df* = 3, and alpha level of .05, in order for χ^2 to be statistically significant, the value must be at least 7.81.

Figure 11.2   Chi-Square Distribution Curve

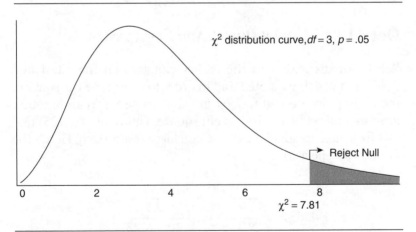

Step 3. Calculate chi-square

(Again, in reality SPSS will do this for us.) By the way—forgot to tell you: we surveyed 200 students in our cafeteria survey at Westside School, and found the following *observed frequencies:*

Observed	75	40	30	55
Expected	50 (1/4)	50 (1/4)	50 (1/4)	50 (1/4)

Yikes, let's look at the formula!!!

$$\chi^2 = \sum \frac{(f_o - f_e)^2}{f_e}$$

$$= \frac{(75 - 50)^2}{50} + \frac{(40 - 50)^2}{50} + \frac{(30 - 50)^2}{50} + \frac{(55 - 50)^2}{50}$$

$$= \frac{625}{50} + \frac{100}{50} + \frac{400}{50} + \frac{25}{50}$$

$$= 12.5 + 2 + 8 + .50$$

$$= 23$$

The obtained chi-square value of 23 is certainly beyond the critical region (which began at 7.81). So far, so good!

Oops! Let's Check Power and Effect Size

Recall our discussion in the earlier chapters on the *t* test and ANOVA in which we stated that in order to determine the *power* of the finding, we needed to look at *effect size* (E.S.). Yeah, another formula and set of levels. For chi-square, values of .10, .25, and .40 are said to be small, medium, and large respectively. Here's the formula for effect size:

$$E.S. = \sqrt{\frac{x^2}{N + x^2}} = \sqrt{\frac{23}{200 + 23}}$$

$$= \sqrt{\frac{23}{223}} = \sqrt{0.93} \approx .321$$

Good! A medium-to-strong effect size.

Step 4. Make a Decision

Since the chi-square value of 23 is well into the critical region, we can conclude that our four menu items are not equally important when students select their lunch options. Instead, there are very significant differences among the four lunch items. We also note that the observed frequencies of both hot dogs and hamburgers were below the expected frequencies, with pizza only slightly above (55/50). Interpreting the results of the chi-square analysis, we can be reasonably confident in saying that our students clearly preferred the salad bar over the other three items (now, I have to figure out how to present this finding to the board without all this statistical mumbo jumbo).

COMMUNICATION OF STATISTICS

As mentioned earlier in the chapter, I am the first to admit that educational leaders must be careful of how data analysis is explained. Though the "salad bar" study mentioned was a serious and legitimate study, I was careful in how I presented the findings to the cafeteria manager, and especially to the members of the board of education. I try not even to use the word *statistics*. We educators have our fear and misinterpretation of statistics; our stakeholders and clients (teachers, parents, and board members) have theirs. So, what would you say to them?

First of all, there was a second part to this study that helped everyone see the outcome, and the effectiveness of the salad bar. I was also concerned about the amount of food wasted each day in our cafeteria. You can imagine the cost! And as you may know, we were one of the very few districts with our own food service operation—most have their food services contracted and outsourced. Regarding the waste issue, I found that there was essentially *no waste* with food items on the salad bar—all items were saved and placed in containers in the walk-in freezer each day. For example, the lettuce was not thrown away—but wrapped and stored for the next day. This was not the case for the food items served on the regular menu. Hot dogs, hamburgers, and pizza could not be stored—so each day, a large amount of food on the regular menu was wasted.

So, when I began to have discussions with our stakeholders about the study, it was reinforced by the food waste issue, giving more evidence that we ought not discontinue the use of the salad bar. Yes, they knew we conducted a survey of 200 students; yes, they knew we analyzed the results; and yes, they knew we had some conclusive evidence to support our case. But, did we talk about chi-square, degrees of freedom, effect size and power, distribution curves and critical regions, .05 significance level, and so on? Certainly not. But with the results of the study and the additional evidence, we had a pretty convincing position to make some sound economical (and educational) decisions about a school service facility.

I think you get my point here. Repeating an earlier statement: The essence of research and data analysis is not statistical tests; the essence is the interpretation and communication of the results. Visit http://www.schoolsanddata.org for a more thorough position paper on the communication of statistics.

CONCLUSION

The chi-square test for goodness of fit is an appropriate test to use if our data are not the usual interval type data, but rather, categorical data. An easy guide is to consider any data consisting of frequencies or counts as categorical. Obviously, much of this kind of data exists in your schools, so the chi-square test is likely to be very useful to you.

However, as always, some cautions. For the chi-square test to be meaningful, it is necessary that each person or response only be counted once in the frequency table. In other words, using our cafeteria example, a student cannot offer more than one choice—his or her response can only be represented in one of the cells. A second requirement is that expected frequencies must be greater than 5 in each cell of the table. If less than 5, there is a loss of statistical power and effect, resulting in a less-than-dependable test result. Finally, we should keep in mind that nonparametric tests such as the chi-square test are not as sensitive as parametric tests; nonparametric tests are more likely to fail to detect a real difference between two treatments. If your data offer a choice, always use a parametric test over a nonparametric test. But, as we have discovered in this chapter, often we do not have a choice between the two, and must use a test such as the chi-square.

APPLICATION ACTIVITY

You have been struggling to find a good book to use for a new professional development session, entitled "Preparing for School Emergencies," to be presented to your teachers next year. To help with your decision, you have asked your present teachers to review three books you have found and identify which one they prefer. The distribution of your teachers' preferences is as follows:

Book 1	Book 2	Book 3
43	25	31

Use a chi-square test and alpha level of .05 to determine if these responses indicate any significant preferences among the three books. And if so, how would you communicate this finding to your teachers without "boring" them with the statistical analysis?

NCLB ACTIVITY

One of the NCLB important goals is, "By 2012–2014, all students will be proficient in reading by the end of the third grade." You have been charged with monitoring and addressing this goal, and with preparing a strategic plan of how to accomplish this goal by 2007 or sooner. As part of your plan, you want to track the progress of your three ethnic groups (which NCLB requires) in reading proficiency from year to year, as measured by pass/fail on your district assessment. Following are data from last year and this year's passing rate. How can a chi-square test help you in your strategic plan?

Passing Rates on District Reading Assessment

	White (%)	Hispanic (%)	Black (%)
2005	85	75	78
2006	90	80	80

CHAPTER TWELVE

The Other "Q"

Yes, it is probably a surprise to you that I devote a whole chapter to something called *qualitative*, and to how we can answer some of our research questions without using means, standard deviations, sum of squares, *t* tests, or ANOVAs. The more time I spend in schools and university preparation programs, the more I am convinced of the importance and power of considering data that have been traditionally deemphasized because they do not consist of raw numbers such as district and state test scores, graduation rates, Scholastic Aptitude Test scores, and student attendance rates.

To help introduce this chapter, and before I provide a working definition of "qualitative study," I want to draw attention to Jonathan Kozol and his seminal book, *Savage Inequalities* (1992). You've read it, I am sure. In his book, Kozol describes the conditions existing in our large urban inner-city schools. To collect his data, Kozol actually lived in these communities, interviewing teachers, principals, students, parents, religious leaders, and other community members. He highlighted such conditions as (1) school buildings without water, heat, and electricity, (2) the absence of adequate books and materials for students and teachers, and (3) poorly prepared teachers and principals in overcrowded schools and classrooms. To many of us who work in more affluent suburban schools, Kozol's work provided our first realization of the poor conditions of our inner-city schools and communities. I suggest that, in many ways, his book was *society's* first realization of the "savage inequalities" existing in our inner-city schools.

GETTING AT THE DEFINITION OF *QUALITATIVE*

The point is that Kozol did not collect and analyze large amounts of test scores, attendance data, and dropout figures. He investigated inner-city schools from a perspective that Creswell (1998) states as "the researcher [as] an instrument of data collection in a natural setting, who gathers words and pictures, then analyzes them inductively, focusing on the meaning of the participants, and describes a process that is expressive and persuasive in language" (p. 14).

Creswell goes on to say that "qualitative research is the study of things or people in their natural settings, attempting to make sense of or interpret phenomena in terms of the meanings people bring to them" (p. 15). The process uses a variety of data collection methods, including observations and interviews to draw a holistic picture of a social or human problem.

It is difficult to define *qualitative* without asking, "How does it differ from *quantitative?*" As we shape and refine our conceptualization of *qualitative* further, perhaps Ragin (1987) can help. He characterizes a key difference: quantitative researchers work with a few variables and many cases, whereas qualitative researchers only use a few cases and many variables.

OK, BUT HOW ABOUT A REAL-LIFE EXAMPLE?

Let me use a personal experience to help us further understand, at least conceptually, the applicability of using qualitative strategies in our work in schools. A few years ago, I was a professor of teacher education at the University of Wyoming's Casper Campus. Obviously, much of my work involved supervising student teachers. One of my students was assigned to an elementary school called Wood's Learning Center. I was immediately struck by the fact that the Wood's Learning Center did not have a principal. Yes, that's right—no principal. I need to give a brief explanation.

The Natrona County School District (Casper and surrounding areas) solicited proposals from teachers for the establishment of innovative school structures. Sort of like "charter" or "magnet" schools. A few years before my arrival at the University of Wyoming, a group of teachers and community members proposed the Wood's

Learning Center to the district's board of trustees. The board approved. The school *is structured* with many innovative and non-traditional components (I use present tense, since the Wood's Learning Center is still in operation today, as described here). The duties of the traditional principal are spread out and shared by the teachers. For example, one teacher handles the budget and financial obligations. Another two teachers are in charge of discipline. Two teachers plan and organize the professional development activities. Still another works directly with scheduling activities for parents. You get the picture—the teachers basically took on all of the responsibilities of the traditional school principal. I imagine one of their motives for doing so was to save the cost of a principal's salary and use it in other ways.

Observing a Phenomenon in Its Natural Setting

As stated before, because of my experience as a school principal and superintendent, I was especially interested in the absence of a principal. And, since I was a fledgling professor (in need of research and writing for tenure and promotion purposes), and since I was in the school 1–2 days per week, I decided to study and investigate the leadership of Wood's Learning Center. I did not realize it at the time, but I set up a situation in which I would be conducting *qualitative* research—with observations, interviews, pictures, and actually "placing myself in the environment." Hmmm . . . sort of what Jonathan Kozol did!

Here is what I was really interested in. We are in agreement that school administration consists of two components: (1) management and (2) leadership. You know, management is making sure the buses run on time, books are delivered to teachers, computers are in good working order, and so on. Leadership, on the other hand, deals with creating a school culture, establishing and sustaining a vision, effectively communicating with staff, teachers, and community, and the like. My real research question was, "In a school without a principal, were both management and leadership evident and being practiced?" My hunch was that the teachers viewed the role of the principal entirely as a management issue (budget, discipline, supplies, parent meetings, and so on).

I'll try to get on with this example and cut to the chase here! To look for the answer to my research question, I needed to talk with people and I needed to observe (just hang around). Keep in mind that this process took more than a year (yep, one of the requirements of good qualitative study). I wasn't particularly interested in test scores, attendance data, or dropout rates. I wanted to find out if "effective leadership," as defined by the literature and practiced in preparation programs, was taking place in a school that purposely chose not to have a principal.

Several patterns or themes surfaced in my study. In talking with teachers, students, and parents, I found that all of the components of leadership associated with management existed at the Wood's Learning Center. The buses did roll on time, the budget was balanced, teachers had textbooks and supplies, students were very orderly and were disciplined appropriately, and they were happy and productive. From all indications, students were achieving at high levels, and the board and community were happy with the school.

Here are some patterns or themes that related to what we commonly refer to as "leadership issues":

1. One parent confessed to frustration when coming to school with a problem and not knowing who to talk with. She later found out that two teachers were handling the lunch-room discipline, but they were in class when she came to school to discuss a problem.

2. Responding to parent interviews, some parents believed that when they had a specific concern about an issue, it was difficult to identify the staff person in charge of that area (for example, a problem occurring on the playground or bus). In addition, upon identifying the staff member in charge, it was difficult to talk with that person immediately, since he or she was in the classroom with students. The issue often had to wait until lunch or after school, or be placed on the agenda for the weekly staff meeting.

3. *Management* as defined (the day-to-day operation of the school) seemed to be sufficiently covered by the teacher teams. However, *leadership* as defined (fostering purpose, passion, and imagination) was less apparent.

4. The existing conception of a school principal was not consistent with today's common view of the principal as instructional leader. As I talked with many teachers, parents, and school board members, a principal image appeared characterized as a manager rather than an instructional leader. The

image also emphasized administrative control and authority. The sense was that those interviewed did not view the role of the principal as one focused on teaching and learning. Quite the contrary, there were indications that some viewed the principal as someone who might actually impede teaching and learning. The former superintendent stated:

> Our concern was that any of our current principals would actually be counterproductive to the proposal made by the teachers. Each of them would have problems with shared decision making and empowering the teachers and parents.

5. The connection of school goals and objectives to district goals appeared weak and unimportant. Though there was a common direction and focus, the relationship to district goals seemed nonexistent. Little collaboration existed between the local school and the district office. A principal stated:

> I do not believe there is effective leadership at the school. They seemed to be doing their own thing, and not concerned with the overall mission and goals of the district. Though they have a teacher who attends administrative meetings, how can that person have time to promote the direction of the district and teach in the classroom also?

A significant and recurring pattern appearing in the data analysis was a common perception of the principal. The teachers, parents, and students interviewed described a *principal* as a person responsible for discipline, scheduling, and finances. This perception seemed based on mechanical control and maintenance. Absent was any mention of the principal as educator: one who directs teaching and learning. Absent also was any mention of the principal as a person who directs efforts to improve student learning and creates a positive school climate.

CONCLUSION

First of all, I am not certain that I could have collected the information just presented in quantitative ways. There just weren't data available to get at the results I found through interviews, focus groups, and observations. The research on school-based management and shared decision making reveals disappointing results of the success of these reforms (Mirel, 1994; Weise, 1995). Many new decision-making structures have led to disaster (Beadie, 1996). One of the most significant studies of decision making in the schools (Weise, Cambone, & Wyeth, 1992) looked at the shared governance structures of 45 schools across the country. The recurring theme across the schools studied was the confusion over who actually had the final word when it came to accepting and implementing a decision. In every case but one, the push toward innovation came from the principal. It was not the inclusion of teachers in the decision-making process that precipitated reform, but the commitment of the principals to change the way the school operated (Weise, 1995).

Again, I do not see how I could have uncovered this *evidence* in a quantitative way. Interviews and observations were necessary to get at the real "under the surface" situation. I hope this example has drawn attention to the importance of "the other Q." And, I hope you include qualitative data collection and analysis in your work with *Schools and Data.*

APPLICATION ACTIVITY

Qualitative researchers strive for "understanding" that comes from interviewing or visiting personally with people related to the field of study. For example, let's suppose you want to know what teachers think about the ongoing "controversy about teacher pay and benefits" being discussed by the superintendent and board of education. So you decide to conduct some individual interviews and small focus groups to get at the real story.

In your interviews and focus groups, how do you know that the teachers' responses are "believable, accurate, and right"? In other words, how can you "cross-check" or "triangulate" the responses to ensure their accuracy? Test scores are test scores are test scores— but, when asking people for their views, how can we be confident of their accuracy?

NCLB ACTIVITY

A specific goal of the No Child Left Behind (NCLB) law states that "all students will be educated in learning environments that are safe, drug free, and conducive to learning." OK, but let's be realistic.

How do we know what a safe learning environment is? I suspect your response will be different from mine—and my response different than my colleague's. And, what is your definition of "conducive to learning"? I suspect it's different than mine.

OK, what am I getting at? I am not convinced that we have any quantitative data that helps us with these questions. For example, what data would we have that "identifies a safe learning environment"? And what data would we have collected that would help us with identifying a "drug-free" environment? Does it mean that we have no evidence of marijuana use but some students smoke cigarettes? Or does it mean that there are no incidents of smoking on campus but we realize that smoking at home occurs?

My point is that I am not sure we have those data available—and that we would need to utilize qualitative methods (or at least mixed methods) to get at the information we need to be able to address the NCLB goal of "students will be educated in learning environments that are safe, drug free, and conducive to learning."

So, develop a strategy for collecting qualitative data that gives you a base or benchmark for pursuing the NCLB goal. How will you determine if an environment is "drug free"? How will you determine if a learning environment is "safe"? And how will you determine if an environment is "conducive to learning"?

CHAPTER THIRTEEN

Putting It All Together

An Evidence-Based Practice Field

I n earlier chapters, I emphasized that educators rarely examine the data existing in schools to assess in a systematic way the quality of teaching and learning in our schools. Much of the fault lies with our universities and their failure to adequately prepare teachers and administrators to deal effectively with data (and evidence). I agree totally with Holcomb's (2005) contention that existing programs at the university level (and the course delivery of statistics and tests and measurement classes) have created a structure that emphasizes esoteric experimental designs that cannot be replicated in a normal school setting. I also echo Bracey's (1997) belief that in all too many instances we teach statistics and other data-related courses in a theoretical manner based on hard-to-understand formulas and far too many examples unrelated to the daily life of educational practitioners.

Yes, I agree that much progress has been made since the first edition of *Schools and Data* was published in 2001. But a new problem has surfaced! In our response to the recent accountability movement (for example, No Child Left Behind [NCLB]), we need to be careful that we do not "just collect data for the sake of collecting data." And let's focus our attention beyond the data to look closely at the *evidence.* I have related my thoughts on *data* versus *evidence* in earlier chapters. And for the second edition of *Schools and Data,* I have changed the subtitle and focus of this chapter from "A Data-Driven Practice Field" to "An Evidence-Based Practice Field."

WHY THE CHANGE TO EVIDENCE-BASED DECISION MAKING?

Data-based decision making is the current buzz term in education circles today. But since the publication of the first edition of *Schools and Data,* I have come to be concerned that not only do we disagree on the meaning of data-based decision making, but that our confidence in data analysis in our schools is mistaken. Let me explain my position further.

I use as an example elsewhere (Creighton, 2005) the comparison of attendance rates with absence rates. You are familiar with the term *average daily attendance* (ADA). We collect these data for several reasons, but primarily they are used to determine the number of dollars we receive in state and federal monies. Simply put, if students are present, schools receive additional funding to help educate them. In addition, schools are now given accountability ratings (NCLB Act) based upon ADA. So principals and superintendents give heavy emphasis on implementing strategies to keep attendance rates high.

Many of the schools receiving the highest accountability rating ("Exemplary") report ADA in a range of 92% to 98%. A 92% sounds pretty good and even has a connotation of a grade of A, right? So we, as school administrators, report that on average, we have a 92% attendance rate.

We have accurately reported the data—*but,* the evidence reveals something completely different and troublesome. If the average daily attendance rate is 92%, what is the average daily absence rate? Well, that's easy—8%. Investigating a little further, we discover that if, on average, 8% of our students are absent, and based on a year of 180 days of instruction, students on average are missing approximately 2 weeks of school per year (8% of 180 equals 14.4 days). Basing a school's Exemplary rating on 92% attendance is one thing, but students on average missing 2 weeks of school each year is quite another matter. You may argue that focusing on attendance is no different than focusing on absence. Well, it is all a matter of perspective, and reflects the difference between *data-driven decision making* and *evidence-based decision making*. Reporting on attendance is a matter of reporting the data. The absence rate is evidence that is not reported or considered to be existing data. I also argue that by looking at the evidence rather than the data, we are more likely to touch more of our *marginal* students—those placed at risk of educational failure. Often, these students are not represented in the data. For example, when we report attendance rates or graduation rates, missing are students not in attendance and students not graduating.

This is my concern now—and the reason for my new approach in this second edition. We have been quick to report the data—and that's good. But in our haste to look at the data, we have been missing the more important evidence. I will not belabor this point further, but do reference a more detailed treatment of my position in *Leading From Below the Surface* (2005), also published by Corwin Press. You can access this book by visiting the *Schools and Data* Web site at: http://www.schoolsanddata.org.

PRACTICE AND PERFORMANCE FIELDS

For some time, I have studied the work of Daniel Kim (1995), an organizational consultant and public speaker who is committed to helping problem-solving organizations transform into learning organizations. Kim is a colleague of Peter Senge (*The Fifth Discipline*, 1990) and cofounder of the MIT Organizational Learning Center, where he is currently the director of the Learning Lab Research Project.

Kim (1995) argued that the accelerated pace of change has overwhelmed our ability to keep up with and understand how these changes affect our organizations. We lack a place to practice decision making where we can make mistakes and step out of the system temporarily so that we can work "on the system" and not just "in the system." He calls this kind of a place a "managerial practice field."

Think for a minute about our jobs in education. Except for a brief experience with some sort of internship or student teaching (both of which continue to suffer from a lack of quality and relevance), where and when do we get an opportunity to leave the day-to-day pressures temporarily and enter a different kind of space in which we can practice and learn? Think another moment about your limited training and preparation in the use of data and evidence to improve decision making. What has been missing? The opportunity or place does not exist where aspiring teachers and administrators can improve their skills in problem analysis, program and student evaluation, data-based and evidence-based decision making, and report preparation. The central idea here is that a *leadership practice field* provides an environment in which prospective school leaders can experiment with alternative strategies and policies, test assumptions, and practice working through the complex issues of school administration in a constructive and productive manner.

I can think of no other profession that does not value or provide opportunities for new professionals to practice in a different kind of space, where one can simply practice and learn. When practicing a symphony, the orchestra has the ability to *slow down* the tempo in order to practice certain sections. A medical student in residence has the opportunity to *slow down* and practice certain medical diagnoses and procedures. The New York Knicks spend most of their time in a practice field, slowing down the tempo, and practicing certain moves, strategies, and assumptions. All of these practice fields exist in an environment with opportunities for making mistakes, in a "safe-failing space to enhance learning" (Kim, 1995).

Let me return to the work of Daniel Kim for a moment.

> Imagine you are walking across a tightrope stretched between two large buildings. The wind is blowing and the rope is shaking as you inch your way forward. One of your teammates sits in the wheelbarrow you are balancing in front of you, while another perches on your shoulders. There are no safety nets, no harnesses. You think to yourself, "One false move and the three of us will be taking an express elevator straight down to the street." Suddenly, your trainer yells from the other side, "Try a new move! Experiment! Take some risks! Remember, you are a learning team!" (Kim, 1995, p. 353)

Kim argued that although this may sound ludicrous, it is precisely what many companies expect their management teams to do: experiment and learn in an environment that is risky, turbulent, and unpredictable. Unlike a high-wire act, a sports team, musician, or physician, however, management teams do not have a practice field in which to learn; they are nearly always on the performance field.

Replace the words *management teams* with *principals* or *school leaders* in the preceding paragraph. Will you not agree that our jobs in education resemble the *risky, turbulent,* and *unpredictable* analogy described by Kim?

An Evidence-Based Practice Field

It is my desire in this final chapter to provide you with a "practice field" designed around the actual work we do in schools. This practice field will also give you the opportunity to practice each of the data analysis strategies discussed in earlier chapters. In addition, you will have the opportunity to experiment with alternative strategies, test some of your assumptions, and practice working with the data found in your schools.

One of the goals of this chapter is to provide a *real enough* practice field so that the activities are meaningful to you as an educational leader but also *safe enough* to encourage experimentation and learning. My hope is that you will be able to step out of the day-to-day pressures faced in your workplace (or your graduate research class) and spend time in the practice field. Musicians practice. World-class athletes practice. But educators, for the most part, are constantly performing.

Again, part of the problem relates to teacher and administrator preparation programs at the university level. Because I am more familiar with and involved in administrative preparation, allow me to make a few comments. Murphy and Forsyth (1999) reported that although supervised practice could be the most critical phase of the administrator's preparation, the component is notoriously weak. Along with other educational leaders (Griffiths, 1999; Milstein, 1990), Murphy claims that field-based practices do not involve an adequate number of experiences and are arranged on the basis of convenience. I am not happy to report that since the first edition of *Schools and Data*, not much has changed. Yes, there are bright spots on the horizon; yes, there are new and innovative approaches to the preemployment experiences of the school leader. But, the bright spots are few—and are the exception rather than the rule. So, here we are again—five years later, and facing the same dilemma of not providing the appropriate preparation for principals and other school leaders in the important work of evidence-based decision making.

I also believe that many of our individual courses in research and statistics should have a practice field where educators can apply what they learn away from the pressures of day-to-day school business. What follows is an attempt to place you in such a practice field. *Try a new move! Experiment! Take some risks! Remember, you are a learning team!*

Horizon High School: A Practice Field

Using the data found in Resource E, create a file titled "Horizon High School Data." The data represent 100 students in Grades 9 through 12. Though the data are fictitious, the variables and entries represent the same kind of data found in your schools. Table 13.1 displays the variables and coding used.

Table 13.1   Coding of Variables for Horizon High School

Gender	Gender of the student: 1 = male, 2 = female
Ethnicity	Ethnicity of the student: 1 = White, 2 = Hispanic, 3 = Black
Freeredu	Qualification for free/reduced lunch: 1 = yes, 2 = no
Math	Standardized test scores in math
Language	Standardized test scores in language
Science	Standardized test scores in science
Writing	District-created writing assessment scores
Grade	Present grade level of student
GPA	Current grade point average of student

Activity 1. Frequency Distributions and Cross-Tabulation

With the use of frequency distributions and cross-tabulations in SPSS or Excel, we would like to take a quick glimpse of the Horizon High School student body. For example, we want to first know:

1. The number of males and females

2. The ethnic makeup of the school

3. The number of students qualifying for free or reduced lunch

4. The number of students in each grade

Though you may not consider the number of males and females or the ethnic makeup of the school to be terribly important, the information regarding ethnicity and free or reduced lunches is used for most of your funding formulas, grant applications, and state and federal reimbursements.

You might want to obtain a graphic representation of your frequency distributions for Horizon High School. Simply select **Chart**, and then select the desired form, such as **Bar Chart**. *Experiment with several different kinds.*

Questions

1. Is there anything unusual about the number of boys qualifying for free or reduced lunch compared to the number of girls? For what reasons might this information be relevant or helpful?

2. Does the gender representation seem normal for an average high school? Is there any weighted effect between gender and any of the other variables?

Discussion

Tables 13.2, 13.3, and 13.4 display some of the information that we need to address these questions.

Table 13.2   Gender of Horizon High School Students

Gender	Number	%	Cumulative %
Male	53	53	53
Female	47	47	100
Total	100	100	

Table 13.3   Gender of Horizon High School Students by Free or
             Reduced Lunch Qualification

Gender	Free or Reduced Lunch?		
	Yes	*No*	*Total*
Male	13	40	53
Female	19	28	47
Total	32	68	100

Table 13.4   Ethnicity of Horizon High School Students

Ethnicity	Number	%	Cumulative %
White	56	56	56
Hispanic	28	28	84
Black	16	16	100
Total	100	100	

Examining data by the use of frequency distributions and tabulation tables allows us to determine very quickly and easily what our population or sample looks like. Such information as gender, race, age, and socioeconomic status is helpful *before* we proceed with further investigation.

Activity 2. Measures of Central Tendency and Variability

You serve as the chairperson of the Horizon High School Curriculum Committee. The director of secondary education in your district has just notified you that she wants a recommendation from you and the committee for this year's textbook adoption. As is the practice at Horizon High School, the board of education only allows one subject area to have new textbooks annually. You and your committee must decide which subject area would benefit most from receiving this year's new textbooks.

Looking at the standardized test scores and the district writing assessment, can you use the measures of central tendency and variability to help you and your committee make a wise decision (based on the evidence) and recommendation to the director of secondary education?

Questions

1. Based on the standardized test data you have for Horizon High School, what subject area might you and your committee recommend for new textbooks this year? And what reasons would you give for your decision?

2. The mean and standard deviation of which subject area might concern you? Approximately 68% of your students scored between what two points in that same subject area? Does it perhaps make sense that the standard deviation on this subject area might be higher than in other subjects? Why or why not?

Discussion

Table 13.5 displays some of the information to address the questions above.

Table 13.5   Horizon Students' Descriptive Statistics of Test Score Data

Subject	N	Minimum	Maximum	Mean	SD
Math	100	234	263	246.86	7.69
Language	100	232	260	248.26	6.38
Science	100	220	276	245.41	8.51
Writing	100	175	234	205.76	11.88

We do notice that the mean scores for the writing assessments are much lower (on average) than those for other subject areas. In addition, the standard deviation is higher than the others, meaning that the writing scores are a bit more spread out from the mean. Specifically, we say that approximately 68% of the high school students scored between 194 and 218 on their writing assessment scores. The standard deviation is 11.88 (rounded to 12), and the mean is 205.76 (rounded to 206). The 12 points represent one standard deviation unit, and we know that approximately 68% of the distribution (students) falls between one standard deviation unit below the mean and one standard deviation unit above the mean.

The scores of the other subject areas are noticeably higher and the standard deviations are a bit smaller, indicating that those scores are centered a little more closely around the mean. Though we need to take many more factors into consideration (evidence), the writing scores give us reason to perhaps suggest new instructional textbooks for that subject area.

Activity 3. A One-Sample *t* Test

The national testing service responsible for publishing your standardized tests states that the average score across the nation on the mathematics assessment is 240. Your principal has asked you to prepare a report to the Horizon Board of Education and wants you to specifically address the progress of your high school students in mathematics. Can you use a one-sample *t* test to help you with your report?

Remember, a one-sample *t* test is a procedure used to determine if the mean of a distribution (your students) differs significantly from a preset value. In other words, does the mean of the Horizon High School math scores differ significantly from the preset value of 240, which represents the national average? As an appropriate test for significance, the one-sample *t* test compares a sample mean with a single fixed value.

Questions

1. Are the Horizon High School students' scores significantly different (higher or lower) from the national average as measured by the standardized math assessment you currently use?

2. Using the same national average score of 240, what can you say about your high school students in other subject areas?

Discussion

Figure 13.1 displays information helpful in addressing the Horizon School Board regarding the math achievement of your high school students. This table is a result of an SPSS one-sample *t* test. Notice that you first get a printout of the descriptive statistics (*N*, mean, and standard deviation). The second printout has the important information we need. Good news for you, your students, and the school board. This one-sample *t* test indicates that the mean score for your high school students in math is 245.55, and is significantly higher than the national average of 240. Remember, on first glance, you might say, "well certainly they are higher." But the real issue and question is, Is the difference large enough to be considered statistically significantly different. This is really based on the sample size (100, *df* 99) and the alpha level we choose as criteria (*p* = .05).

Figure 13.1 One-Sample *t* Test for Math Scores

One-Sample Statistics

	N	Mean	Std. Deviation	Std. Error Mean
math	100	245.55	8.674	.867

One-Sample Test

	Test Value = 240					
					95% Confidence Interval of the Difference	
	t	df	Sig. (2-tailed)	Mean Difference	Lower	Upper
math	6.398	99	.000	5.550	3.83	7.27

With an alpha level of .05 and 99 degrees of freedom (*N* −1), the *t* value required for significance is approximately 1.9, as shown in Resource B. You notice from your SPSS test report that the *t* value is actually 6.4 (rounded), with a significance much lower than our targeted .05. Though SPSS reports .000, we recall that this figure is rounded to three decimals, so we can report *p* < .001. This level is well into the critical region required to reject the null hypothesis of no significant difference between your high school students and the national average.

Figure 13.2   SPSS One-Sample *t* Test for Writing Scores

One-Sample Statistics

	N	Mean	Std. Deviation	Std. Error Mean
writing	100	205.85	11.892	1.189

One-Sample Test

	Test Value = 240					
					95% Confidence Interval of the Difference	
	t	df	Sig. (2-tailed)	Mean Difference	Lower	Upper
writing	−28.717	99	.000	−34.150	−36.51	−31.79

Using a one-sample *t* test to compare the national average of 240 with the other subject areas reveals that both science and language means are also significantly higher than the national average. However, you will notice that the one-sample *t* test for writing reveals that the mean score is significantly *lower* than the national average, as shown in Figure 13.2.

This draws attention to why we want to conduct a two-tailed test. We are interested in *any difference*—higher or lower. In this case, the significance is equally important to know. The board of education will no doubt feel pretty good about what is happening in math, language, and science. But, the evidence reveals a problem with writing—and you have some evidence-based decisions to make before discussing this finding with them. Maybe you have a high population of limited-English speakers; maybe the difference relates to the kind of performance students are asked to complete on their writing exam; or maybe it is gender specific (females with high scores and males with very low scores), skewing the mean downward? Do some more investigating to see if you can find further *evidence* explaining this particularly troublesome finding.

Activity 4. An Independent-Samples *t* Test

You have taught high school algebra, geometry, and trigonometry for more than 10 years at Horizon High School and currently serve as department chair. Though your superintendent has tried to recruit a woman or two for the math department, the department continues to be dominated by male instructors. With the increased attention on Title IX, social justice, and gender equity, educators must be sensitive to and aware of the issues of gender equity in both academic and extracurricular activities.

A local parent activist group has approached your school board and made the claim that because of the dominance of male math instructors, males are receiving better instruction and more attention in math courses than are the female students. Specifically, these parents claim that boys are outperforming girls in math achievement.

Your superintendent has asked you to report your assessment of the situation at the Friday afternoon faculty meeting. Use an independent-samples *t* test with a significance level of .05 to help prepare for the Friday meeting.

Questions

1. Do the males and females differ significantly from each other on standardized math test performance?

2. What unusual finding presents itself, and how might you explain this finding to the faculty and superintendent on Friday?

3. How might you use evidence-based decision making to address the general issue of gender equity at Horizon High School?

Discussion

As displayed in Figure 13.3, we find there is a 3.41 mean difference between the means (males = 243.94; females = 247.36).

Hmmm . . . Actually, we discover that the girls are outperforming the boys in standardized math scores. Careful, let's check the power of this finding. Again, the real question is, Is the difference large enough to be statistically significant? Yes, the *t* value is −1.996, with a significance level of .049. By-the-book significant, but look how close we are to .05. This finding is too close to call significant. But, good news—there does not seem to be enough *evidence* to conclude that there is any difference academically in math between girls and boys. So, I would feel good about the fact that math achievement is pretty balanced in terms of gender performance.

Figure 13.3 Independent-Samples *t* Test: Gender and Math Scores

Group Statistics

	male=1,female=2	N	Mean	Std. Deviation	Std. Error Mean
math	male	53	243.94	8.798	1.208
	female	47	247.36	8.253	1.204

Independent-Samples Test

		t	df	Sig. (2-tailed)	Mean Difference
math	Equal variances assumed	−1.996	98	.049	−3.418

What kinds of further investigations or decisions would you want to consider with your faculty? And even with the gender finding, is this *proof* that gender and math achievement are not problem areas? And what about this perception that your parent group had about male math instructors? Are there perhaps other variables or factors at play here? Evidence-based decision making!

Activity 5. A GPA Analysis

As a guidance counselor at Horizon High School, you spend considerable time advising seniors about attending college. Your local university just announced that it is raising the grade point average (GPA) entrance requirement from 2.8 to 3.0.

Questions

1. Can you produce from the Horizon High School data file an analysis of your seniors' GPA in relation to the newly announced GPA requirement by the university?

2. If you analyzed the GPA scores across all grade levels, what concerns might you have?

Discussion

I threw an easy one at you for a change of pace. This issue can be addressed with a single cross-tabulation, as shown in Table 13.6.

Table 13.6   Horizon High School Grade Level by GPA

	GPA								
Grade	2.5	2.8	2.9	3.0	3.1	3.2	3.3	3.4	Total
9	1	8	3	7	9		5		33
10	3	4	6	3	8		2		26
11	7	10		3					20
12			4	7	5	2	1	2	21
Total	11	22	13	20	22	2	8	2	100

Things look pretty good with our seniors' GPAs. All but four seniors have GPAs of 3.0 or higher, and those four have GPAs that are very close (2.9). Perhaps we might want to provide some intervention to the four who are "on the bubble." Or perhaps they are students planning on attending the local community college for 2 years before transferring to the university, in which case the issue is not so serious.

Wow! The number of students in Grades 9, 10, and 11 with noticeably low GPAs is somewhat alarming. Slightly more than 30% of the ninth graders, 50% of tenth graders, and 85% of eleventh graders have GPAs below 3.0. Of special concern is the large group of eleventh graders, for they only have 1 year to improve significantly. Again, lots of opportunities for *evidence-based decision making.*

Activity 6. One-Way Analysis of Variance

Having had a close call with the local activist parent group over gender equity issues, you, as the Horizon High School principal, decide that you want to look at any significant differences in math scores among the three ethnic groups at your school. In other words, you are interested to see whether any of your three ethnic groups (White, Hispanic, and Black) differ significantly from each other in the subject area of math.

A one-way analysis of variance (ANOVA) will help address this concern. The ANOVA will reveal any significant differences within any of the comparisons of the three ethnic groups and their respective math scores. In this case, the dependent variable is the math test and the independent variables are the three ethnic groups. Recall that the ANOVA indicates only *whether* there is any difference among the three groups—it does not identify the exact location of any difference. We will need to select a post hoc test (Tukey HSD) to help answer that question.

The requirement for a *t* test is that we can compare *only* two means—it is the ANOVA that allows us to compare many means at one time. The means for the math scores for each of the ethnic groups will be compared with each other: Whites with Hispanics, Whites with Blacks, Hispanics with Blacks. The one-way ANOVA will generate a significance value indicating whether there are significant differences within the comparisons being made. The significance value does not indicate where the difference is or what the differences are, but the post hoc test will help identify pairwise differences.

Questions

1. After running a one-way ANOVA on math scores, run another for each of the other subject areas.

2. With the help of the Tukey HSD test, where does the problem seem to lie?

Discussion

I will not display all of the tables from this analysis. Figure 13.4 displays some important descriptive statistics, an analysis of ethnic groups and math, and the Tukey HSD test.

First of all, we realize that the group sizes are unequal in this analysis. In other words, it would be better if all three ethnic groups consisted of similar numbers of students. Admitting a weakness of our study, let's look at the results. The ANOVA reveals a significant difference (or differences) within comparisons of math scores and the three ethnic groups, based on $F (2, 97) = 3.743$, $p = .027$. You notice that the significance level is .027, much lower than the selected criteria of .05, making the finding somewhat more powerful.

Now let's see if we can specifically identify *where* the significant difference is. Looking at the Tukey HSD test, and focusing on the "Multiple Comparisons" printout in Figure 13.4, we see significant difference *only* in two places: comparing Whites with Blacks and

Figure 13.4 One-Way ANOVA and Tukey HSD for Ethnicity and Math

ANOVA

math

	Sum of Squares	df	Mean Square	F	Sig.
Between Groups	533.732	2	266.866	3.743	.027
Within Groups	6915.018	97	71.289		
Total	7448.750	99			

Multiple Comparisons

Dependent Variable: math
Tukey HSD

(I) white=1, black=2, hispanic=3	(J) white=1, black=2, hispanic=3	Mean Difference (I–J)	Std. Error	Sig.	95% Confidence Interval	
					Lower Bound	Upper Bound
White	Hispanic	−3.696	1.954	.147	−8.35	.96
	Black	−5.786(*)	2.393	.046	−11.48	−.09
Hispanic	White	3.696	1.954	.147	−.96	8.35
	Black	−2.089	2.646	.710	−8.39	4.21
Black	White	5.786(*)	2.393	.046	.09	11.48
	Hispanic	2.089	2.646	.710	−4.21	8.39

* The mean difference is significant at the .05 level.

Homogeneous Subsets

Tukey HSD

white=1, black=2, hispanic=3	N	Subset for alpha = .05	
		1	2
White	56	243.59	
Hispanic	28	247.29	247.29
Black	16		249.38
Sig.		.262	.648

Means for groups in homogeneous subsets are displayed.
a. Uses Harmonic Mean Sample Size = 25.846.
b. The group sizes are unequal. The harmonic mean of the group sizes is used. Type I error levels are not guaranteed.

comparing Blacks with Whites (really the same comparison, but in reverse, causing one value to be positive and the other to be negative). Notice the significance value next to the comparison: Whites and Blacks show .046. OK, significant, but really pretty close to .05—this finding is not as powerful, so we must be careful in our interpretation. But suffice it to say that we have a significant difference—reflecting back to earlier chapters, we likely have a *practical significance* here rather than a strong significant difference.

Though there are differences between the mean scores of Whites and Hispanics and between Hispanics and Blacks, they are not significant (.147 and .710), being much greater than the selected criteria of .05.

The last printout displayed in Figure 13.4 is one of homogeneous subsets. This analysis places like sets together (little difference) and unlike (difference) sets apart. So we see here that Subset 1 consists of Whites and Hispanics and Subset 2 consists of Hispanics and Blacks. The Hispanics' mean is close to the Whites', but also shares closeness with the Blacks'. What this really means is that the greatest difference is between the Whites and Blacks—*but*, nonetheless, there is also less difference among the Hispanics and Whites and Blacks. Sounds confusing, perhaps, but we see a very serious pattern of concern here. There are disparities among all three groups, though one more serious than the others. We must investigate further to see what we might be able to do in regard to curriculum and instruction to reduce or eliminate these disparities among ethnic groups and math achievement. More *evidence-based decision making!*

Activity 7. Two-Way Analysis of Variance

Analysis of variance looks for significant differences between groups by comparing the means of those groups with some selected variable. In the one-way ANOVA described in Activity #6, we were interested to see if the three ethnic groups differed from each other on their performance on standardized math assessment scores. The one-way part of the analysis indicates that there is only one independent variable (the ethnic groups) and only one dependent variable (math scores).

The two-way ANOVA allows us to use two independent variables. We are now interested to discover if there is a relationship (as measured by math scores) between ethnic group and gender (two independent variables). The two-way ANOVA will allow us to determine if gender or ethnic group or an interaction between gender and ethnic group has an effect on math achievement.

Questions

1. Do females and males differ significantly in math performance as measured by standardized test scores? This question addresses the *main effect* for gender.

2. Do students in the three ethnic groups differ significantly in
   math performance as measured by standardized test scores?
   This question addresses the *main effect* for ethnic group.

3. Is there an interaction between gender and ethnic group?
   This question addresses the possibility, as an example, that
   Hispanic females score higher in math but White females
   score lower.

Discussion

Figure 13.5 displays descriptive statistics and the ANOVA tests
of between-subjects effects.

Let's use the information in Figure 13.5 to answer the three
questions posted at the beginning of Activity #7:

1. There is no statistically significant main effect for gender.
   Females (mean = 247.36) did not score significantly higher
   than males (mean = 243.94), $F = .74$, $p = .405$.

2. There is no significant main effect for ethnicity. Though the
   test did not meet the criteria of .05 significance level, .077
   is not too distant. Again here, we may want to emphasize
   practical significance. Blacks had higher math scores in both
   the male and female categories. However, the difference is
   not considered significant because the difference was not
   great enough to meet our selected .05 criteria.

3. There is no statistically significant *interaction* between gender and ethnicity, $F = .242$, $p = .781$. Actually, this is good
   news. Math performance seems to be consistently similar
   across gender and ethnic groups. If this were not the case,
   we would have cause for greater alarm.

Activity 8. Pearson Correlation

I saved the last activity in the evidence-based practice field for
last, since I want to make the point that much of what we do in

Figure 13.5 Two-Way ANOVA for Ethnicity, Gender, and Math Scores

Descriptive Statistics

Dependent Variable: math

male=1, female=2	white=1, black=2, hispanic=3	Mean	Std. Deviation	N
male	White	242.57	8.218	37
	Hispanic	245.60	10.319	10
	Black	249.67	8.262	6
	Total	243.94	8.798	53
female	White	245.58	9.483	19
	Hispanic	248.22	5.847	18
	Black	249.20	9.578	10
	Total	247.36	8.253	47
Total	White	243.59	8.701	56
	Hispanic	247.29	7.659	28
	Black	249.38	8.823	16
	Total	245.55	8.674	100

Tests of Between-Subjects Effects

Dependent Variable: math

Source	Type III Sum of Squares	df	Mean Square	F	Sig.
gender	53.194	1	53.194	.740	.392
ethnic	379.338	2	189.669	2.639	.077
gender * ethnic	35.707	2	17.854	.248	.781

a. r^2 = .093 (Adjusted r^2 = .045)

schools can be addressed or answered with correlations. Though there are several analyses we can conduct, let's take a look at whether or not there might be a correlation among our four subject areas (math, science, language, and writing). The specific questions might be:

1. Do our students seem to perform similarly in the four subject areas across subjects? In other words, do students who score high in math also have a tendency to score high in science (and any other combination of comparisons)? This answer to this type of question would be revealed by a positive correlation coefficient (for example, $r = .67$).

2. Do our students seem to perform dissimilarly in the four subject areas across subjects? In this case, we are interested to see if, for example, students who score high in math might have a tendency to score lower in language or writing. The answer to this kind of question might result from a negative correlation coefficient (for example, $r = -.65$). If one set of scores tends to be high, while another set of scores goes down, there is a negative correlation.

Figure 13.6 displays the Pearson correlations for our students and their four subject area scores. Remember, the cells that show 1 are simply a correlation of the same variable (that is, math correlated with math). We disregard these cells. Also, be aware that each cell is repeated—because of the order of the variables being correlated (for example, math with science is no different than science with math).

Figure 13.6   Math, Science, Language, and Writing Correlation

Correlations

		math	language	science	writing
math	Pearson Correlation	1	−.004	.004	.004
	Sig. (2-tailed)		.969	.971	.967
	N	100	100	100	100
language	Pearson Correlation	−.004	1	.334(**)	.183
	Sig. (2-tailed)	.969		.001	.068
	N	100	100	100	100
science	Pearson Correlation	.004	.334(**)	1	.252(*)
	Sig. (2-tailed)	.971	.001		.011
	N	100	100	100	100
writing	Pearson Correlation	.004	.183	.252(*)	1
	Sig. (2-tailed)	.967	.068	.011	
	N	100	100	100	100

* Correlation is significant at the 0.05 level (2-tailed).
** Correlation is significant at the 0.01 level (2-tailed).

We see several things of interest. First, the largest and statistically significant relationship exists between science and language ($r = .334$, $p = .001$). This means that as students tend to score (up or down) in science, they have a strong tendency to score in the same direction in math. You notice SPSS places two stars next to the coefficient if it meets the more stringent criteria of .001. Not sure what this may mean at this point—but you need to think about why this might be the case.

Second, we see another significant correlation—between science and writing ($r = .252$, $p = .011$). Again, this correlation is positive, so it means that as students tend to score (up or down) in science, they have a similar tendency in writing. Not quite as strong as the language and science, but still significant at the .05 significance level.

We will not go further here—but you see there are many other observations we can make with this particular analysis that will help us with more *evidence-based decision making.* For example, we would assume that students who score well in language would also have a tendency to score well in writing. With our 100 students, this is not the case, as there is not noticeable or significant correlation in that direction. Really, the lack of a correlation means that there is no pattern between these two subject areas. Hmmm. We might want to investigate this situation further. We might want to discuss collaborative cross-curricular activities with our two faculty teaching writing and language—or if the same instructor teaches both, are both subjects being included in the curriculum? Just an idea!

CONCLUSION

Argyris and Schoen, in their book *Organizational Learning* (1978), stated that people function with a gap between their espoused theories (what they believe to be the right course of action) and their theories in use (what they choose to do given the surrounding circumstances). Sound like our life in the schools? I think so. The authors continue by saying that failure to recognize and close those gaps impedes organizational learning.

The evidence-based practice field can help close some of those gaps. A crucial component, however, is the opportunity to take what has been learned in the practice field and apply it to the real life of the school and the community. So creating practice fields is important but is in itself inadequate (Kim, 1995). There is danger in allowing practice fields to become training grounds as an end in themselves. The learning experiences are no better than the old traditional ways of doing things if they are not moved and adapted to the workplace.

I continually state that the real culprits in this dilemma are the university teacher and administrator preparation programs. Though there are a few "bright spots" in some preparation programs, for the most part there is not a substantive attempt to increase teachers' and administrators' understanding of data analysis or the use of analysis to improve real teaching and learning.

Gravetter and Wallnau introduced their excellent book *Statistics for the Behavioral Sciences* (2000) by asking their readers to read the following paragraph, which was adapted from a psychology experiment by Bransford and Johnson (1972). I would like to use the same exercise as a conclusion to this book:

> The procedure is actually quite simple. First you arrange things into different groups depending on their makeup. Of course, one pile may be sufficient, depending on how much there is to do. If you have to go somewhere else due to the lack of facilities, that is the next step; otherwise you are pretty well set. It is important not to overdo any particular endeavor. That is, it is better to do too few things at once than too many. In the short run this may not seem important, but complications from doing too many easily arise. A mistake can be extensive as well. The manipulations of the appropriate mechanisms should be self-explanatory, and we need not dwell on them here. At first, the whole procedure will seem complicated. Soon, however, it will just become another facet of life. It is difficult to foresee any end to the necessity of this task in the immediate future, but then one never can tell. (Gravetter & Wallnau, 2000, p. 4)

Perhaps the quoted paragraph sounds like some complicated statistical procedure. But it actually describes the everyday task of doing laundry. Knowing this, now go back and read the passage again.

The authors' purpose, like mine here, was to point out the importance of context. When things are out of context, even the simplest procedures can seem complex and difficult to understand. I suggest that this has been one of the problems with the instructional delivery of data-related courses in teacher and administrator preparation programs. They lack context and applicability.

I presented in the Preface four important weaknesses of data analysis as presented in most teacher and administrator preparation programs: (1) the irrelevance of statistics to the day-to-day lives of principals and teachers; (2) the lack of integration of technology into the teaching and learning of statistics; (3) the inappropriate design of statistics courses for teachers and administrators; and (4) the overemphasis of data analysis for research projects and dissertations. I wanted to present a slightly different approach to data analysis in this book. I attempted to emphasize the importance of descriptive analysis and shift the use of inferential analysis from the traditional research and dissertation model to one of more relevance and applicability to teachers and administrators.

I firmly believe that until we begin to seriously evaluate and analyze the existing data in our schools, our profession will continue to be scrutinized and questioned with regard to student achievement and quality teaching and learning. As stated earlier in this second edition, there has been much progress in this area over the last few years, but think for a moment! The cry of alarm from our communities, legislators, and business leaders has not diminished since the first edition of *Schools and Data* in 2001. There is still much work to be done. There is some evidence that we are losing some of our market share to private schools, vouchers, charter schools, and some emerging for-profit enterprises (Holcomb, 2005). We must discontinue the practice of making decisions based upon intuition and gut feelings. And we must guard against looking only at existing data—and look more closely at related evidence below the surface.

I sincerely hope this book, and especially the evidence-based practice field, helped to make you more comfortable and familiar with the data found in your school. In addition, I hope you see how you can use these existing school data to assist in making sound educational decisions about teaching, learning, and assessment.

I invite you to communicate with me regarding *Schools and Data* by visiting the accompanying Web site at: http://www.schools anddata.org.

Resource A:
Music Correlation

Students	Band	Math	Language	Science
1	3.0	220	215	220
2	4.0	240	210	225
3	2.5	210	250	235
4	2.0	215	230	210
5	4.0	260	240	220
6	3.0	230	270	250
7	3.5	240	240	220
8	4.0	259	220	240
9	3.0	245	230	250
10	4.0	280	270	230
11	4.5	300	260	220
12	2.0	230	250	225
13	3.0	250	245	235
14	4.0	275	235	210
15	2.5	200	260	220
16	2.0	200	255	250
17	4.0	290	250	220
18	3.0	250	230	240
19	3.5	270	245	250
20	4.0	280	270	230
21	3.0	260	270	260
22	4.0	270	250	230
23	4.5	310	260	280
24	2.0	170	250	220

Resource B:
The t Distribution Table

Alpha Level

df	0.50	0.20	0.10	0.05	0.02	0.01
1	1.000	3.078	6.314	12.706	31.821	63.657
2	0.816	1.886	2.920	4.303	6.965	9.925
3	0.765	1.638	2.353	3.182	4.541	5.841
4	0.741	1.533	2.132	2.776	3.747	4.604
5	0.727	1.476	2.015	2.571	3.365	4.032
6	0.718	1.440	1.943	2.447	3.143	3.707
7	0.711	1.415	1.895	2.365	2.998	3.499
8	0.706	1.397	1.860	2.306	2.896	3.355
9	0.703	1.383	1.833	2.262	2.821	3.250
10	0.700	1.372	1.812	2.228	2.764	3.169
11	0.697	1.363	1.796	2.201	2.718	3.106
12	0.695	1.356	1.782	2.179	2.681	3.055
13	0.694	1.350	1.771	2.160	2.650	3.012
14	0.692	1.345	1.761	2.145	2.624	2.977
15	0.691	1.341	1.753	2.131	2.602	2.947
16	0.690	1.337	1.746	2.120	2.583	2.921
17	0.689	1.333	1.740	2.110	2.567	2.898
18	0.688	1.330	1.734	2.101	2.552	2.878
19	0.688	1.328	1.729	2.093	2.539	2.861
20	0.687	1.325	1.725	2.086	2.528	2.845
21	0.686	1.323	1.721	2.080	2.518	2.831
22	0.686	1.321	1.717	2.074	2.508	2.819
23	0.685	1.319	1.714	2.069	2.500	2.807
24	0.685	1.318	1.711	2.064	2.492	2.797

df	0.50	0.20	0.10	0.05	0.02	0.01
25	0.684	1.316	1.708	2.060	2.485	2.787
26	0.684	1.315	1.706	2.056	2.479	2.779
27	0.684	1.314	1.703	2.052	2.473	2.771
28	0.683	1.313	1.701	2.048	2.467	2.763
29	0.683	1.311	1.699	2.045	2.462	2.756
30	0.683	1.310	1.697	2.042	2.457	2.750
40	0.681	1.303	1.684	2.021	2.423	2.704
50	0.679	1.296	1.671	2.000	2.390	2.660
60	0.677	1.289	1.658	1.980	2.358	2.617
120	0.674	1.282	1.645	1.960	2.326	2.576

Resource C:
The F Distribution Table

Table entries are critical values for the .05 level of significance.

Denominator: df	Numerator: df									
	1	2	3	4	5	6	7	8	9	10
1	61	200	216	225	230	234	237	239	241	242
2	18.51	19.00	19.16	19.25	19.30	19.33	19.36	19.37	9.38	19.39
3	10.13	9.55	9.28	9.12	9.01	8.94	8.88	8.84	8.81	8.78
4	7.71	6.94	6.59	6.39	6.26	6.16	6.09	6.04	6.00	5.96
5	6.61	5.79	5.41	5.19	5.05	4.95	4.88	4.82	4.78	4.74
6	5.99	5.14	4.76	4.53	4.39	4.28	4.21	4.15	4.10	4.06
7	5.59	4.47	4.35	4.12	3.97	3.87	3.79	3.73	3.68	3.63
8	5.32	4.46	4.07	3.84	3.69	3.58	3.50	3.44	3.39	3.34
9	5.12	4.26	3.86	3.63	3.48	3.37	3.29	3.23	3.18	3.13
10	4.96	4.10	3.71	3.48	3.33	3.22	3.14	3.07	3.02	2.97
11	4.84	3.98	3.59	3.36	3.20	3.09	3.01	2.95	2.90	2.86
12	4.75	3.88	3.49	3.26	3.11	3.00	2.92	2.85	2.80	2.76
13	4.67	3.80	3.41	3.18	3.02	2.92	2.84	2.77	2.72	2.67
14	4.60	3.74	3.34	3.11	2.96	2.85	2.77	2.70	2.65	2.60
15	4.54	3.68	3.29	3.06	2.90	2.79	2.70	2.64	2.59	2.55
16	4.49	3.63	3.24	3.01	2.85	2.74	2.66	2.59	2.54	2.49

Denominator: df	Numerator: df									
	1	2	3	4	5	6	7	8	9	10
17	4.45	3.59	3.20	2.96	2.81	2.70	2.62	2.55	2.50	2.45
18	4.41	3.55	3.16	2.93	2.77	2.66	2.58	2.51	2.46	2.41
19	4.38	3.52	3.13	2.90	2.74	2.63	2.55	2.48	2.43	2.38
20	4.35	3.49	3.10	2.87	2.71	2.60	2.52	2.45	2.40	2.35
21	4.32	3.47	3.07	2.84	2.68	2.57	2.49	2.42	2.37	2.32
22	4.30	3.44	3.05	2.82	2.66	2.55	2.47	2.40	2.35	2.30
23	4.28	3.42	3.03	2.80	2.64	2.53	2.45	2.38	2.32	2.28
24	4.26	3.40	3.01	2.78	2.62	2.51	2.43	2.36	2.30	2.26
25	4.24	3.38	2.99	2.76	2.60	2.49	2.41	2.34	2.28	2.24
26	4.22	3.37	2.98	2.74	2.59	2.47	2.39	2.32	2.27	2.22
27	4.21	3.35	2.96	2.73	2.57	2.46	2.37	2.30	2.25	2.20
28	4.20	3.34	2.95	2.71	2.56	2.44	2.36	2.29	2.24	2.19
29	4.18	3.33	2.93	2.70	2.54	2.43	2.35	2.28	2.22	2.18
30	4.17	3.32	2.92	2.69	2.53	2.42	2.34	2.27	2.21	2.16
32	4.15	3.30	2.90	2.67	2.51	2.40	2.32	2.25	2.19	2.14
34	4.13	3.28	2.88	2.65	2.49	2.38	2.30	2.23	2.17	2.12
36	4.11	3.26	2.86	2.63	2.48	2.36	2.28	2.21	2.15	2.10
38	4.10	3.25	2.85	2.62	2.46	2.35	2.26	2.19	2.14	2.09
40	4.08	3.23	2.84	2.61	2.45	2.34	2.25	2.18	2.12	2.07
42	4.07	3.22	2.83	2.59	2.44	2.32	2.24	2.17	2.11	2.06
44	4.06	3.21	2.82	2.58	2.43	2.31	2.23	2.16	2.10	2.05
46	4.05	3.20	2.81	2.57	2.42	2.30	2.22	2.14	2.09	2.04
48	4.04	3.19	2.80	2.56	2.41	2.30	2.21	2.14	2.08	2.03
50	4.03	3.18	2.79	2.56	2.40	2.29	2.20	2.13	2.07	2.02
60	4.00	3.15	2.76	2.52	2.37	2.25	2.17	2.10	2.04	1.99
70	3.98	3.13	2.74	2.50	2.35	2.22	2.14	2.07	2.01	1.97
72	3.96	3.10	2.72	2.47	2.32	2.00	2.11	2.03	1.99	1.94

Resource D: Chi-Square Distribution Table

	Alpha Level
df	*0.05*
1	3.841
2	5.991
3	7.815
4	9.488
5	11.071
6	12.592
7	14.067
8	15.507
9	16.919
10	18.307
11	19.675
12	21.026
13	22.362
14	23.685
15	24.996
16	26.296

	Alpha Level
df	*0.05*
17	27.587
18	28.869
19	30.144
20	31.410

Resource E:
Horizon High School Data

Students	Gender	Ethnic	Freeredu	Math	Language	Science	Writing	Grade	GPA
1	1	1	1	234	248	239	175	9	2.8
2	2	2	2	239	242	242	188	11	2.5
3	1	2	1	263	258	263	200	12	3.0
4	2	1	1	244	244	239	212	10	2.8
5	1	2	1	247	243	245	196	9	2.8
6	2	1	1	257	259	247	198	9	3.0
7	1	1	2	239	252	244	211	11	2.8
8	1	2	1	248	252	243	187	12	3.2
9	2	1	1	247	249	253	221	12	3.1
10	1	1	2	234	245	239	190	10	3.1
11	2	3	2	247	248	247	222	11	2.8
12	1	3	1	247	254	242	214	10	2.5
13	1	1	2	239	240	245	197	10	3.0
14	1	3	1	247	247	236	190	9	3.1
15	2	1	2	247	232	244	189	9	3.3
16	2	3	1	263	240	239	187	9	3.0
17	1	2	2	244	242	242	211	11	2.8
18	2	3	1	247	250	263	214	12	3.0
19	1	2	1	257	248	276	221	10	2.9
20	1	1	2	239	250	245	189	9	3.1
21	1	1	2	248	259	247	190	9	2.8
22	2	2	1	247	252	244	214	11	2.5
23	1	1	2	234	252	266	234	12	3.2
24	2	2	2	247	249	253	212	12	3.1
25	2	2	2	247	240	239	189	10	2.8

Students	Gender	Ethnic	Freeredu	Math	Language	Science	Writing	Grade	GPA
26	2	1	1	239	248	247	198	11	3.0
27	2	2	2	247	254	242	211	10	2.8
28	1	1	1	247	240	267	214	10	2.9
29	2	1	1	234	247	236	189	9	2.9
30	1	3	1	239	249	244	190	9	3.1
31	2	3	1	263	240	239	189	9	2.8
32	1	1	2	244	242	242	214	11	2.5
33	1	2	2	247	258	263	199	12	3.0
34	2	2	1	257	244	239	212	10	3.1
35	1	1	2	239	243	245	197	9	2.5
36	2	3	1	248	259	247	198	9	3.0
37	1	1	2	247	252	244	211	11	2.8
38	1	1	1	234	252	239	214	12	3.4
39	1	1	1	247	249	253	221	12	3.1
40	2	2	2	247	256	239	231	10	3.1
41	2	1	2	239	247	247	222	11	2.8
42	1	2	2	247	254	242	214	10	2.5
43	2	1	1	255	240	256	213	10	3.0
44	1	3	2	263	247	236	189	9	3.1
45	1	1	2	244	256	244	200	9	3.3
46	1	1	2	247	240	239	196	9	3.0
47	2	2	1	257	242	242	211	11	2.8
48	1	1	2	239	258	263	214	12	2.9
49	2	2	2	248	244	239	221	10	2.9
50	2	2	2	247	243	245	201	9	3.1

Students	Gender	Ethnic	Freeredu	Math	Language	Science	Writing	Grade	GPA
51	2	2	1	234	259	247	203	9	2.8
52	2	1	2	239	252	244	214	11	2.5
53	1	1	1	263	252	220	217	12	3.0
54	2	1	1	244	249	253	212	12	3.1
55	1	1	1	254	256	239	216	10	3.3
56	2	3	1	257	248	247	198	11	3.0
57	1	2	1	239	254	242	211	10	3.1
58	1	1	2	248	240	240	214	10	2.9
59	2	1	2	247	247	236	189	9	2.9
60	1	1	1	234	240	244	187	11	3.1
61	2	3	1	233	240	239	200	12	2.8
62	1	1	2	247	242	242	214	10	2.5
63	1	2	1	239	258	263	211	9	3.0
64	1	1	1	222	244	239	212	9	3.1
65	2	3	2	247	243	245	199	11	3.3
66	2	1	2	221	259	247	198	12	3.0
67	1	1	2	232	252	244	211	12	2.8
68	2	2	1	255	252	254	214	10	2.9
69	1	2	2	225	260	253	221	11	2.9
70	1	1	2	239	245	239	231	10	3.1
71	1	1	2	248	248	247	222	10	2.8
72	2	2	1	250	254	242	214	9	2.5
73	1	1	2	234	240	245	197	9	3.0
74	2	2	2	247	247	236	190	9	3.1
75	2	2	2	247	245	244	200	11	3.3

Students	Gender	Ethnic	Freeredu	Math	Language	Science	Writing	Grade	GPA
76	2	1	1	239	240	239	198	12	3.0
77	2	1	2	247	242	242	211	10	2.8
78	1	1	1	250	258	263	214	9	3.4
79	2	1	1	250	244	239	221	9	2.9
80	1	1	1	245	243	245	186	11	3.1
81	2	1	1	263	259	247	199	12	2.8
82	1	1	2	244	252	244	214	12	2.5
83	1	1	2	247	252	240	213	10	3.0
84	2	1	1	257	249	253	212	11	3.1
85	1	1	1	239	250	239	200	10	3.3
86	2	3	2	248	248	247	198	10	3.0
87	1	1	1	247	254	242	211	9	2.8
88	1	1	2	234	240	238	214	9	2.9
89	1	3	1	255	247	236	200	9	2.9
90	2	1	2	247	245	244	198	11	3.1
91	2	3	2	239	240	239	211	12	2.8
92	1	3	1	247	242	242	214	10	2.5
93	2	1	1	250	258	263	198	9	3.0
94	1	1	2	263	244	239	212	9	3.1
95	1	1	1	244	243	245	200	11	3.3
96	1	1	2	247	259	247	198	12	3.0
97	2	2	1	257	252	244	211	12	2.8
98	1	1	2	239	252	260	214	10	3.3
99	2	2	2	248	249	253	221	11	2.9
100	2	2	2	247	238	239	202	10	3.1

References

Argyris, C., & Schoen, D. (1978). *Organizational learning: A theory of action perspective.* Reading, MA: Addison-Wesley.

Beadie, N. (1996). From teachers as decision makers to teachers as participants in shared decision making: Reframing the purpose of social foundations in teacher education. *Teachers College Record, 98*(1), 77–103.

Bracey, G. (1997). *Understanding educational statistics: It's easier (and more important) than you think.* Arlington, VA: Educational Research Service.

Bransford, J., & Johnson, M. (1972). Contextual perquisites for understanding: Some investigations of comprehension and recall. *Journal of Verbal Learning and Verbal Behavior, 11,* 717–772.

Creighton, T. (1999). Standards: The Idaho horizon. *Perspectives [Idaho Association of School Administrators], 16*(4), 8–13.

Creighton, T. (2001). *Schools and data: The educator's guide for using data to improve decision making* (1st ed.). Thousand Oaks, CA: Corwin Press.

Creighton, T. (2005). *Leading from below the surface.* Thousand Oaks, CA: Corwin Press.

Creswell, J. (1998). *Qualitative inquiry and research design: Choosing among five traditions.* Thousand Oaks, CA: Sage.

Field, A. (2005). *Discovering statistics using SPSS for Windows.* Thousand Oaks, CA: Sage.

Fitch, M., & Malcom, P. (1998). Using data effectively for school improvement planning. *Effective School Report for Research and Practice, 16*(6), 1, 4–5.

Gravetter, F., & Wallnau, L. (2000). *Statistics for the behavioral sciences.* Belmont, CA: Wadsworth.

Griffiths, D. (1999). *Educational administration: Reform PDQ or RIP* (Occasional Paper No. 8312). Tempe, AZ: University Council for Educational Administration.

Holcomb, E. (2005). *Getting excited about data: How to combine people, passion, and proof.* Thousand Oaks, CA: Corwin Press.

Kim, D. (1995). Managerial practice fields. In S. Chawla & J. Renesch (Eds.), *Learning organizations: Developing cultures for tomorrow's workplace* (pp. 131–152). Portland: Productivity Press.

Kozol, J. (1992). *Savage inequalities: Children in America's schools.* New York: Crown.

McNamara, J. (1996). *Teaching statistics in principal preparation programs.* College Station: Texas A & M University, Research Department.

Milstein, M. (1990). Rethinking the clinical aspects of preparation programs: From theory to practice. In S. L. Jacobson & J. A. Conway (Eds.), *Educational leadership in an age of reform* (pp. 119–130). New York: Longman.

Mirel, T. (1994). School reform unplugged: The Bensinville New American School Project. *American Educational Research Journal, 31,* 481–515.

MPR Associates, Inc. (1998). *At your fingertips: Using everyday data to improve schools.* Brisbane, CA: George Lithograph.

Murphy, J., & Forsyth, P. (1999). A decade of change: An overview. In J. Murphy & P. Forsyth (Eds.), *Educational administration: A decade of reform* (pp. 3–38). Thousand Oaks, CA: Corwin Press.

Picciano, A. (2005). *Data-driven decision making for effective school leadership.* Upper Saddle River, NJ: Merrill Prentice Hall.

Ragin, C. (1987). *The comparative method: Moving beyond qualitative and quantitative strategies.* Berkeley: University of California Press.

Runyan, R., Haber, A., & Coleman, K. (1994). *Behavioral statistics: The core.* New York: McGraw-Hill.

Senge, P. (1990). *The fifth discipline: The art and practice of the learning organization.* New York: Doubleday.

Sprinthall, R. (2000). *Basic statistical analysis.* Boston: Allyn and Bacon.

Terozzi, G. (2005, September). High school reform: Examining local and state efforts. *NASSP Newsleader, 85,* 1–2.

U.S. Department of Education. (2001, January). *Conference Report to H.R. 1, The No Child Left Behind Act.* Washington, DC: Author.

Weise, C. (1995). The four "I's" of school reform: How interests, ideologies, information, and instruction affect teachers and principals. *Harvard Educational Review, 65*(4), 571–592.

Weise, C., Cambone, J., & Wyeth, A. (1992). Trouble in paradise: Teacher conflicts and shared decision making. *Educational Administration Quarterly, 28,* 350–367.

Index

Absence rate data, 10–11,
    156–157
Accountability, 156
Alpha levels
    analysis of variance (ANOVA),
        107–108, 117–118
    basic concepts, 35
    distribution table, 180–185
    error rates, 102–103
    F distribution, 107–108
    independent-samples *t* test,
        85, 90, 92–93, 97–98
    one-sample *t* test, 78
    Z scores, 71–75
Analysis of variance (ANOVA)
    independent measures
        analysis of variance, 60,
        98, 102–114, 169–172
    repeated measures analysis of
        variance, 116–122
    two-way analysis of variance,
        127–136, 172–173, 174
Application activities
    analysis of variance
        (ANOVA), 113
    basic data analysis, 7
    chi-square test, 147
    correlation calculations, 49
    data entry techniques, 17
    independent-samples
        t test, 100
    level of significance tests, 80

    measures of central
        tendency, 30
    qualitative research
        methods, 153
    regression analysis, 62
    repeated measures analysis of
        variance, 125–126
    two-way analysis of
        variance, 135
Argyris, C., 176
Attendance data, 2, 9–11,
    156–157
Averages, measures of
    See Central tendency,
        measures of

Bonferroni test
    See Post hoc tests
Bracey, G., 5, 155
Bransford, J., 177

Case studies
    correlation calculations,
        39–45
    statistical analysis usage, 5–7
Categorical data, 46
Cause and effect, 33–34, 133
Central tendency, measures of,
    23–26, 30, 162–164
Chi-square test, xv, 138–147,
    184–185
Collaborative teaching, 47–49

Collection and organization
    techniques, 20–30
Communication skills, 145–146
Companion website, xvi
Confidence levels, 73
Correlation, 32–51,
    173–176, 179
    See also Regression analysis
Creswell, J., 149
Critical regions
    analysis of variance (ANOVA),
        107–108, 117–118
    chi-square test, 142, 143
    independent-samples *t* test,
        90, 92
    one-sample *t* test, 78
    Z scores, 73–75
Cross-tabulation, 23, 160–162,
    168–169

D.A.R.E. Program, 116–125
Data analysis
    See Collection and organization
        techniques; Research
        question formulation;
        Statistical analysis
Data scales, 82–84
Decision-making strategies
    and data analysis, 103–104
    data-driven decision making,
        9, 11, 67–68, 124–125,
        155–157
    evidence-based decision
        making, 98, 155–157,
        160–178
    practice field concept,
        157–160
    and qualitative research
        methods, 149–154
Degrees of freedom (*df*)
    analysis of variance
        (ANOVA), 107
    chi-square test, 142, 143

distribution tables, 180–185
independent-samples *t* test,
    90, 92
one-sample *t* test, 76
repeated measures analysis of
    variance, 117–118
Dependent variables, 64–65, 67
Descriptive statistics, xii–xiii
Distribution curves, 69

Effect sizes, 86–87, 110–111,
    121–122, 144
Errors, 75–76, 85, 88–89,
    103, 140
Eta square, 110
Evidence-based decision making,
    98, 155–157, 160–178
Existing (surface) data, 000
Experimentation strategies
    See Practice field concept

F distribution, 106–109,
    182–183
Focus groups, 000
Forsyth, P., 159
F ratio, 105, 121, 127, 132
Frequency distributions, 21–22,
    25–27, 138–145, 160–162

Grade point average (GPA)
    analysis, 168–169
Gravetter, F., 177

Holcomb, E., 4–5, 155
Homogeneous subsets,
    123–124, 172
Honestly significant difference,
    112–113
Horizon High School activities,
    160–176, 186–190
Hourglass analogy, 66–67
House Committee on Education
    and the Workforce, 31

Hypothesis testing
    analysis of variance (ANOVA),
       104–113, 117–121
    basic concepts, 65–68
    chi-square test, 142–145
    independent-samples *t* test, 85,
       89–93, 96–98
    qualitative research methods,
       150–154
    t statistic, 75–80
    two-way analysis of variance,
       128–134
    Z scores, 70–75
    See also Horizon High School
       activities

Independent measures analysis of
    variance, 60, 98, 102–114,
    169–172
Independent-samples *t* test, 81,
    86–101, 166–168
Independent variables, 64–65, 67
Inferential statistics, xii–xiii
Innovation strategies
    See Practice field concept
Instructional strategies,
    129–133
Integrated curriculum, 47–49
Interaction factors, 129–134
Interval scales, 83, 84, 137
Interviews, 000

Johnson, M., 177

Kim, D., 157–159
Kozol, J., xii, 148–149

Least squares method, 54
Level of significance
    basic concepts, 35
    independent-samples *t* test,
       85, 90, 92–93, 97–98
    one-sample *t* test, 78

Z scores, 71–75
    See also Alpha levels
Line of best fit, 52, 54, 56, 61–62

Main effect, 129–133, 173
Main website, xvi
Mean, measures of, 24, 26, 30,
    68–70
    See also Analysis of variance
       (ANOVA); *t* statistic
Mean square (*MS*), 105–106
Measures of central tendency,
    23–26, 30
Measures of variability, 27–29
Median, measures of, 24, 30
Method of least squares, 54
Microsoft Excel
    analysis of variance (ANOVA),
       110, 111
    basic concepts, 3
    correlation calculations,
       42–44
    data calculations, 24, 26
    data entry techniques, 11–13
    frequency distribution
       calculations, 26–27
    independent-samples *t* test,
       94, 96
    regression analysis, 57–58
    two-way analysis of variance,
       131–132
    usage recommendations,
       19–20
Mode, measures of, 24, 30
Moments, definition of, 34–35
Multiple regression, 51–52
Murphy, J., 159

National Center for Educational
    Statistics (NCES), 4
National Science Foundation
    (NSF), 4
Negative correlation, 34, 36

No Child Left Behind Act (2002)
  analysis of variance (ANOVA)
      activity, 114
  chi-square test activity, 147
  correlation calculation
      activities, 49
  goals, 17–18
  independent-samples *t* test
      activity, 101
  measures of central tendency
      activities, 31
  one-sample *t* test activity, 80
  qualitative research activity,
      153–154
  regression analysis
      activities, 63
  repeated measures analysis of
      variance activity, 126
  two-way analysis of variance
      activity, 135–136
Nominal scales, 83, 137
Nonparametric tests,
      xv, 137, 146
Null hypothesis
  See Hypothesis testing

One-sample *t* test,
      77–79, 164–166
One-tailed tests, 92–93
One-way analysis of variance
  See Independent measures
      analysis of variance
Ordinal scales, 83
Outliers, 38, 86

Parametric tests, xiv–xv,
      137, 146
Pearson correlation coefficient,
      34–37, 41, 44–45,
      56–57, 59, 173–176
Pearson, Karl, 35
Percentages/percentiles, 8–11
Perfect correlation, 34, 36
Picciano, A., 4

Positive correlation, 33–34, 36
Post hoc tests, 111–113, 121,
      122–124, 170–172
Power, concept of, 84–86
  See also Effect sizes
Practical significance,
      72–75, 172, 173
Practice field concept, 157–160
Prediction techniques, 38, 39,
      51–52, 60–61
Preparation programs,
      effectiveness of, x, 148,
      151, 159, 177–178
Probability values, 35, 71–73, 85
  See also Alpha levels

Qualitative methods, 000
Qualitative research methods,
      149–154
Quantitative research
      methods, 149

Ragin, C., 149
Random samples, 84, 86
Ratio scales, 83, 84
Regression analysis, 000, 51–63
  See also Correlation
Repeated measures analysis of
      variance, 116–122
Research question formulation
  analysis of variance (ANOVA),
      104–113, 117–121
  basic concepts, 65–68
  chi-square test, 142–145
  independent-samples
      t test, 85, 89–93, 96–98
  qualitative research methods,
      150–154
  t statistic, 75–80
  two-way analysis of variance,
      128–134
  Z scores, 70–75
  See also Horizon High School
      activities

Risk-taking strategies
    See Practice field concept
Romney, M., 31

Scales, data, 82–84
Scatterplots, 38
Schoen, D., 176
Senge, P., 157
Significant discrepancies
    analysis of variance (ANOVA),
        110–113, 169–172
    chi-square test, 139–145
    correlation calculations,
        173–176
    independent-samples *t* test,
        84–85, 87, 167
    one-sample *t* test, 164–166
    repeated measures
        analysis of variance,
        117–118, 121
    two-way analysis of
        variance, 131–134,
        172–173, 174
    Z scores, 70–75
Simple regression, 51–60
Skewness, 85–86
Spearman correlation, 46
Standard deviation, 26, 27–29,
    69–70, 74–76, 84,
    163–164
Standard error, 75–76, 85,
    88–89
Standardized test scores,
    1, 162–163
Statistical analysis
    basic concepts, 2–3, 81–86
    case studies, 5–7
    importance, 4–5, 87–89
    software programs, 3, 11–17,
        19–20
Statistical Package for the Social
    Sciences (SPSS)
    analysis of variance (ANOVA),
        109–110

basic concepts, 3
correlation calculations,
    44–45
cross-tabulation
    calculations, 23
data calculations, 22–24
data entry techniques,
    11, 13–16
frequency distribution
    calculations, 22
independent-samples *t* test,
    90–94, 95, 99
one-sample *t* test, 78–79
regression analysis, 57–61
repeated measures analysis of
    variance, 118–120,
    123–124
standard deviation
    calculations, 27–29
two-way analysis of variance,
    131–132
usage recommendations,
    19–20

Test scores, 1, 162–163
t statistic
    basic concepts,
        81–86, 105
    distribution table, 180–181
    independent-samples
        t test, 81, 86–101,
        166–168
    multiple sample tests,
        102–103
    one-sample *t* test, 75–80,
        164–166
    requirements, 83–84
Tukey's HSD test, 112–113,
    122–123, 170–172
Two-tailed tests, 92–93,
    94, 96, 166
Two-way analysis of variance,
    127–136, 172–173, 174
Type 1/Type 2 errors, 85

Variability, measures of, 27–29,
    162–164
Variables, relationships of
    correlation analysis,
        32–50
    dependent and independent
        variables, 64–65, 67
    regression analysis, 51–63
Variances
    independent measures
        analysis of variance, 60,
        98, 102–114, 169–172

random samples, 86
    repeated measures analysis of
        variance, 116–122
    two-way analysis of variance,
        127–136, 172–173, 174

Wallnau, L., 177
Websites, xvi, 4
Wood's Learning Center
    (Wyoming), 149–152

Z scores, 68–76

**CORWIN
PRESS**

The Corwin Press logo—a raven striding across an open book—represents the union of courage and learning. Corwin Press is committed to improving education for all learners by publishing books and other professional development resources for those serving the field of PreK–12 education. By providing practical, hands-on materials, Corwin Press continues to carry out the promise of its motto: **"Helping Educators Do Their Work Better."**